A History of

Racism

*My Search for
Atonement,
Understanding, and a
Freed Soul*

J.A. Purvis

ZAUBERHUND

PRESS

Copyright © 2020 J.A. Purvis

ISBN: 9781651740422

Introduction

It's important that you understand I'm not a historian. I'm a carpenter. I'm a carpenter with an academic background in philosophy, psychology, and religion. And I'm a carpenter with a past...a past that – for better or worse – I can document back a few centuries.

The case I'm about to make is largely circumstantial; the evidence, while actual, is sketchy. I've had to correct the record on a few occasions and fill in many blanks with conjecture. Whenever this has been necessary, I've admitted it plainly. No one will be able to accuse me of misrepresenting myself.

This is *my* story, cast against the backdrop of an old family history that many will wish to condemn from the outset. I understand: it's easy to do and very much in fashion. It's far more difficult to cop to being the descendant of plantation-owning slaveholders and to being, at least as an ignorant youth, a racist. But this is a story of evolution and hopefully redemption, a story sadly pertinent to our times.

I don't seek your sympathy, but I do seek your willingness to listen, hopefully without prejudice, a request that could justifiably collapse under its own painful irony. I present my story in the hope that it will facilitate understanding at a moment in our history when understanding is becoming a tragically rare commodity. I seek healing, not only for me but for my country. It's in that spirit that I offer what follows.

A Word About the "N" Word

My children were raised in a language-saturated home; not only did we read to them *before* they were born, we never spoke baby talk or dumbed-down our conversations with them. We didn't purge our discourse of syllables, and they were never taught that certain words were "bad." We *did* teach them that language could be appropriate or inappropriate, and as such, only two terms were forbidden in our home - "goddamn" and "nigger" - since I was unable to imagine any situation in which either might be appropriate.

I've softened my stance since then. First, both of my kids are in their thirties, so my attempting to control what they have to say is pretty pointless; but second, I've concluded that the banned words might indeed have appropriate uses. Among other things, I've discovered that invoking the full and eternal condemnation of the deity is sometimes helpful while trying to remove the lid from a particularly obstinate jar of something, among other things.

But quite frankly, much of the story I'm about to share with you is tragic and ugly, so it should come as no surprise that some of the language needed to tell it will be ugly as well. There are those who believe the word "nigger" should be permanently purged from our lexicon or that, if used, be invoked only by a person of color. Those individuals might endorse the removal of Mark Twain's books from our libraries or Quentin Tarantino's movies from our cinemas. And while I would never claim parity with that heady company, I think exceptions must be made in matters of art.

I'm not attempting to orchestrate shock value and I intend no offense. The strategy of taking offense is often an ill-advised and petulant conversation stopper, an impenetrable barricade erected against the exchange of ideas. Within an artistic context, sometimes the artist's intention is to summon sensations of offense within his audience- consider Picasso's *Guernica* or Serrano's *Piss Christ*. Both are beautiful, yet each invokes a kind of abhorrence.

I struggled mightily with my decision to use a term that I believe is the single most vile expression in our language. Whenever I felt its use was warranted, I sought an alternative way of expressing what needed to be said. I felt ashamed even to type it. But in the end, I made the choice to use it in print…less than twenty times, but in each case I squirmed and resisted. This isn't the only time I'll apologize in this book, but I consider that decision to be proper.

I've had much help along the way. In most cases I've used only first names when citing my references because I have no idea how these individuals might react to my subject or my writing. But, frankly, their feelings were irrelevant from my perspective. I became determined to tell this story and make it public, even though it likely would upset certain parties, notably family members. Some of my research was done surreptitiously, but never deceptively. Any information I gleaned from speaking with others was always done in the full spirit of outright inquiry, although I was admittedly sometimes reluctant to indicate why I was asking. Those chips are going to fall where they may, and I'm willing to accept that responsibility.

Otherwise, I want to thank my editor, Madelyn Morgan and her husband Kevin, who also reviewed my first draft. Madelyn's among the best, and it's a humbling thing to receive an editor's changes and comments. A humbling thing, indeed.

Most especially, I need to thank my ever-resourceful wife, Peggy Ann, who joined me on what must have seemed interminable trips through graveyards and libraries and musty stacks of grimy old documents. I'm pretty sure my obsession with honoring a long-deceased southern slave has mystified her at more than one turn; but every time I announced a new trip out of town or money that I planned to spend, she never blinked an eye, never questioned my motives, never tried to turn me from my goal. She's listened to me for hours on end, as I grew giddy with new discoveries or crushed by new realizations, and she did not once fail to love and support me through it all. She's always been the one burning candle that has illuminated even the darkest of my nights: she is my lodestar, my queen.

J.A. Purvis

June 21, 2019

For I.N.,
and the magnificence you are
and shall become.

-Poppy

Chapter 1

Learning to Fear

My mother was a brilliant woman and a gifted storyteller. Her formal schooling ended with high school and a few courses at the Indiana Business College. She remained the least educated of four siblings, despite generally being regarded as the brightest. She had a brooding, melancholy nature, and battled depression her entire life. When she died in her nineties, she was on no fewer than four antidepressants and anti-anxiety drugs.

In the early 1950's, just about the time I was born, she experienced a severe emotional collapse – a "nervous breakdown" – and was placed under the care of a psychiatrist who recommended she take a job outside our home. Every day she took me to a babysitter and then hopped on the bus downtown, working at one of the large department stores, but her tenure was brief. Just before my fourth birthday, I contracted rheumatic fever and was confined to total bedrest. My feet didn't touch the floor for six months, and she couldn't bear to leave me with caregivers. Her work in retail ended as abruptly as her college career, and she became my doting round-the-clock nurse.

My recollections of that time are vague and gauzy, but I do recall them as happy. I was the youngest of three sons, eight years younger than my closest brother, and my parents did everything they could to keep my active mind and confined body occupied. Friends and relatives often dropped by, usually bringing gifts that were then stored in the coat closet near the couch where I spent my waking hours. As soon as I became bored, the closet door would be flung open and some new wonder presented to me. My best friends, my closest playmates, were stuffed animals and puppets and hobbled pull toys, relieved of their towing strings and rendered as immobile as I was.

I think it was during this time that my mother began entertaining me with her storytelling. She read to me often, sometimes children's books, but generally more adult fare – tales of the Arabian Nights, Aesop, Pegasus and Bellerophon, fantastic stories of children transmogrified into insects. She recited long passages of poetry to me from memory and began teaching me numbers and simple phrases in Latin. She also regaled me with long narratives of heroes and villains, classic fairy tales that never varied one word in her recitation. Her memory was astonishing and remained so until her death.

By far my favorite times were the ones when she recounted her family's – *my* family's - long history. My mother was fiercely proud of her heritage, abundantly festooned with aristocrats, wealthy landowners and entrepreneurs, adventurers and scholars, musicians, writers, and journalists. She could document direct links to George Washington and James

Whitcomb Riley; one of her uncles, a White House correspondent, flew with the Wright brothers. The whole lot of them were educated and erudite and able. Even at the tiny age of four years, I felt myself to be part of a long, proud line, with roots reaching deep into my nation's history. My mother made me understand that we were people who made a difference. Intentionally or not, even at my tender age she made me sense an obligation to antiquity.

She had a soft singsong voice and just the hint of a sloppy lisp, an impediment she shared with her one brother, and I loved the magical times when she spun her long yarns of family adventure. Again, my mother was a brilliant woman and a gifted storyteller. And, at least until very late in her life, she was an incorrigible racist.

She wasn't a militant, raging racist; rather, she was the kind of matter-of-fact racist I've known my entire life, the kind who simply accepts that people of color are of a lower order of being on a *prima facie* basis. For them, black folks are childlike and simple, forever destined to pursue life on a plane substantially beneath that of whites. My mother wasn't a bigot riddled and convulsed with hatred; instead, she was entirely condescending and dismissive.

Occasionally she told of Alexander, an ancestor. After getting into some disagreement with his father and feeling slighted about his inheritance, Alexander left his Virginia home with "his mule and his nigger" (she was quoting from family writ here…maybe her father). The latter was a freed slave named Price who, according to family lore, chose to remain with Alexander after his emancipation, including accompanying Alexander when he traveled west to seek his fortune.

Alexander and Price planned to go to St. Louis but didn't make it. Instead they settled in southern Indiana, and Alexander eventually moved north, establishing a homestead on several acres in both Marion and Johnson counties. I listened transfixed in the gloaming and drifting to sleep as my mother described how the devoted Price stayed with Alexander until his death, when he was laid to rest in the family cemetery. The notion that a black man, a freed slave, was buried along with my ancestors absolutely seized my imagination, just as her stories of Perseus and Medusa did. I wasn't very old at all when I determined to see this man's grave.

My own evolution of racial awareness isn't particularly unique, particularly to people raised in the pre-civil rights era. My childhood world in rural Indiana was almost entirely segregated; the only "nigros" (my mother's term) I ever saw were on television, usually in comic roles. But then there was Jimmy.

Jimmy was a kid who lived near us, a friend of my brothers, and he had an unusually dark complexion. One day when I was probably three years old, I shouted to Jimmy as he got on his bicycle to leave, "Goodbye, black boy!"

There was nothing racist in my salutation: I was three years old and Jimmy looked black to me, but my mother immediately grabbed my arm and jerked me back.

"Don't call him that, ever!" she hissed. I had no idea what I'd done wrong, but apparently calling someone "black" was a horrible insult. I had just received my first lesson in bigotry.

My next recollection of racial consciousness comes from a brief period when my family lived in Hollywood, Florida. My father had always been compulsive, and shortly after my rheumatic fever had abated and I'd been given permission to resume a relatively normal, if restricted, child's life, he came home from work and announced we were moving.

"Even the birds are smart enough to go south," he pointed out. My parents sold our house, crammed much of our belongings into a pathetic box truck parked next to my grandmother's barn, and made the long trek to warmer climes in two cars, my father driving one and my oldest brother the second. Dad had former business associates in Miami who were running a thriving aluminum awning business; he went to work for them and rented a house in Hollywood, a town located halfway between Miami and Ft. Lauderdale.

Florida in the late 1950's was, in a number of ways, the deepest of the Deep South. Certainly, segregation was the status quo in Indiana, but in Florida it was overt and unapologetic. "Whites Only" signs hung over the entrances to many businesses, and several establishments had three restrooms, "Men," "Women," and "Colored." Even in the most extreme cases of need, my mother refused to allow me to use the colored toilet, explaining in near-hysteric terms that it would undoubtedly be filthy.

"They never clean those," she snapped. She was afraid I might become…I don't know, *contaminated*.

We lived in Hollywood only a year or so. Things didn't work out well for dad, and my oldest brother was deeply in love with a girl back in Indiana. They married shortly after our return and have remained so ever since. But it was in Hollywood that I learned the most insidious and intractable lesson of racism. It reverberates in me to this day.

We lived in Hollywood, but there was also *West* Hollywood and, at least as I recall it, West Hollywood was where anyone who wasn't white lived. In Indiana, such hard racial boundaries were common, but the geographical lines weren't so explicit on the map. Everyone knew where "Niggertown" was in Indianapolis, an area my father also occasionally referred to as "the reservation." But down south, these segregated areas were plotted and platted, and any resident of West Hollywood was expected to conduct his business in our town quietly and quickly and then be on his way. Consequently, while I occasionally observed blacks near our home, I never really interacted with them. And I was terrified when I did.

At some point during our residence in Hollywood, it was explained to me – and keep in mind I was only five years old – that all nigros carried knives and would savagely slice me to pieces at the slightest provocation. It was essential then that I avoid them at all costs; if I happened to see a nigro walking on the street, I was to cross to the other side, never making eye contact. And if one should chase me, which if given the opportunity they most undoubtedly would, I was to run up to the first house I saw and enter, regardless of whether I knew the occupant or not. Since this was Hollywood, the people inside would most certainly be white and willing to protect me against the nigro's vicious assault.

The picture painted so vividly for me was that nigros were very much like wild beasts, barely restrained in their behavior at the best of times, always seething beneath the surface and just on the verge of violence against me and all whites. The best policy was simple avoidance, and prudence advised that contact be minimal with them at any time. Certainly, the plan of keeping them all in one segregated municipality made perfect sense, just as one kept dangerous animals locked in a pen.

I'm not certain which of my family members explained all this to me; my vague recollection is that it was one of my brothers, but I hate to make that assertion, since it all seems so reprehensible in hindsight. But there it is: only five years into my life, at the very foundation of my awareness, I became terrified of black people...*all* black people.

We returned to Indiana in 1958. My parents rented half a duplex in an Indianapolis neighborhood populated with transitory white professionals and military people from the nearby navy facility. Dad worked briefly at his old aluminum siding sales job, but soon decided to strike out on his own as a remodeling contractor. He struggled for a number of years to make a success of it, but eventually he was bringing in a solid income, and we purchased a small house on the eastside of town. It was teeming with families just like ours, and as I entered adolescence I spent long summer days among half a dozen other boys my age, all white.

These were times of general racial unrest in our country. The civil rights movement was gaining a foothold in the popular consciousness, and giants of racial equality such as Dr. Martin Luther King Jr. and the Kennedys dominated the news along with reports of riots, sit-ins, and demonstrations. Maybe, because "the colored problem" featured so prominently in the headlines, racist jokes and epithets were commonplace in the conversations of my friends. It's an odd but well-known ironic trait of human nature that when we're confronted with a jarring across-the spectrum institutional change, we often respond culturally with perverse humor; "dead baby" jokes, first popularized in the early 1960's, are thought to be a response to the Supreme Court's decision to legalize abortion. The Beatles' infamous 1966 album cover for *Yesterday and Today* featured the band dressed in what look to be butcher's coats holding dismembered pieces of baby mannequins. I often wonder if the racist content of my comrades' adolescent banter didn't have a similar genesis.

In any case, our everyday talk was riddled with explicitly racist jokes and derisive references. I really hesitate to make specific citations here, but I'm going to, simply to underscore the ugly nature of our language. And the examples I'm about to give are some of the more innocuous ones. There are many I recall that are so hateful that I'll never repeat them ever. I feel a kind of physical sickness in recalling them.

One friend used to say, "There's a nigger in the woodshed" when he suspected one of us to be dissembling or playing fast-and-loose with the truth. If someone behaved in a particularly stupid fashion, he might be accused of being "dumber than a day-old nigger." Anyone who was overly slobbery with a shared cigarette was told he was "nigger-lipping." A poorly cobbled together repair job was "nigger rigged." And so on and so on.

Just as my children's generation invoked "gay" as a

term of derision, my generation said "nigger."* In both cases, labels of disdain originally coined by the privileged referring to the disenfranchised were more generally appropriated as insults. Both are examples of imbecilic ignorance and youthful callousness.

My friends and I had no idea why blacks were inferior and socially ostracized- we simply knew that they were. Our bigotry suffused the atmosphere of our childhood; it was in the air we breathed. It was as certain as the sky above and the earth below. It was the order of things, unquestioned and unchallenged. And that's precisely why, when that order was publicly challenged in the early 1960's, so many of us found ourselves confused and resentful.

In the fourth grade, my classmates and I were subjected to a series of personality inventories and intelligence assessments, and four of us were selected to receive further evaluation, including a one-on-one session with a child psychologist. I remember it as being bizarre. His interview included not only other written tests, but I remember being verbally interrogated and tousled about

*In a Season Three episode of the famous South Park animated series, "Rainforest Shmainforest," a children's chorus sings a perky ditty containing the lyrics, "Let's save the rainforest, whadaya say? Being an activist is totally gay." The reference is anything but laudatory.

by him. He didn't touch me in any inappropriate way, but the fact that he touched me at all always seemed odd.

In any event, based on the sum of the test results, I was invited to attend a school for intellectually gifted kids. I didn't hesitate, and in the fall of 1963 my parents enrolled me in the fifth grade at George Rogers Clark School #1.

Our curriculum was similar to that of other public grade schools with some notable differences. Mostly the material was more in depth and advanced, but we also were taught French, public speaking, and expository writing. I suddenly found myself among a bunch of smart kids. In regular school I'd been at the top of the class, but now I struggled to maintain an even keel in math and science, although I still excelled in reading and writing.

In 1963 our school, nestled along a tiny side street in a middle-class neighborhood, was exclusively white. By the time I graduated in the spring of 1967, it was anything but. The shift in its demographic, which was tidal, began with the Civil Rights Act of 1964, a federal law that suddenly made illegal third bathrooms, "No Colored" establishments, and public discrimination of any kind on the basis of race or religion. One of the more pronounced impacts of the legislation was the rapid disappearance of Niggertown and places like it, all fueled by white fear of the black man and how he would breach the bastions of our racially uncontaminated neighborhoods.

The Jim Crow laws of the south, which guaranteed that whites and blacks would remain separated by statute, hadn't been quite so codified in the northern states. One of the reasons I saw three restrooms in Florida is because the state constitution sanctioned such racial separation. No such constitutional provisions existed in the north, but the practice of segregation was perpetuated by "softer" convention…neighborhood covenants and banking practices and the like.

If property in a given neighborhood could be owned only by whites, and if persons of color weren't permitted to obtain loans at reasonable rates, then one of inevitable results was the founding of Niggertowns and West Hollywoods. These ghettos of rental properties were maintained in the least possible inhabitable standards by their white landlords, all of whom were comfortably ensconced in their pristine communities far from their tenants' squalor. And just as inevitable was the common notion that evolved among whites that black people could never maintain their homes. Never mind that it wasn't actually their property at all. Just look at it! Middle-class whites had all seen what Niggertown looked like, and it didn't resemble our well-manicured neighborhoods at all. It was ramshackle and unkempt and unpainted and littered with uncollected trash. And it looked like that because its real property owners, who were white and invisible, neglected it completely.

But the power of guilt-by-association is strong, and if a hapless white person crossed into Niggertown, he didn't see the multiple layers of ownership and responsibility and negligence. What he saw were black people surrounded by decay and depredation. Broken windows, uncut grass, missing shingles. We kids were terrified – specifically our *parents* were terrified – that if blacks were allowed to escape the confines of their rightful places…well, then, that same sort of desolation would be visited on our own neighborhoods.

Unscrupulous real estate agents smelled panic early in the process after civil rights legislation was enacted. "Blockbusting" was the name given to the strategy they used to frighten white homeowners into selling at below-market prices, only to turn around and sell the very same properties to eager black buyers at inflated prices. "White flight" began as disillusioned and angry whites ran to the suburbs to escape what they saw as the certain collapse of their neighborhoods. "For Sale" signs sprung up in yard after yard, almost overnight, and whole areas changed from white to black in a matter of months. The School #1 neighborhood did.

I didn't live there; since the gifted program was offered in four schools throughout the city, they all drew on multiple townships. My parents drove me to school each day, but several of the kids in my class lived in the area. Sometimes I went home with them after school for a few hours, and I clearly remember one evening when my friend's father spat vitriol. He felt backed into a corner. He was an attorney and an educated man, active in his local church and community organizations. And he was livid.

"I've worked my entire adult life to support my family," he said. "I've put everything into this house: it represents all I've ever accomplished. And now I'm being forced to throw it away." He shook his head.

I followed his angry gaze down the street. It looked to me like every other house was for sale. Some of the signs had diagonal "Price Lowered" banners pasted across them. When he spoke again, his voice was softer and sadder.

"We're going to lose it all. All of it." He went inside and I was left confused, wondering why he'd spoken that way to me. I was a kid. I had nothing to offer him, no condolences, no advice. All I could do was bear witness to his frustration, and I really didn't understand it.

Within weeks, they had moved into a new neighborhood a few miles to the east. The houses were on tiny lots, built with 2x3 framing and clad in thin skins of hastily applied aluminum siding. But his neighbors were all white. Every single one of them.

When I first attended School #1, there were no black kids there. When I left for high school four years later, the whites were a thin minority, most of them in my class.

Arlington High School was big and new, maybe six or seven years old and the flagship of the Indianapolis Public Schools system when I arrived. Its 3400 students, children of fecund suburban baby boomers, matriculated in an enormous complex of dappled concrete walls and sleek aluminum trim. The library was larger and better stocked than many municipal ones; the big, sleek stadium might've been the envy of small colleges. We had a planetarium with a spooky, insect-like Zeiss projector enthroned prominently in its center. The administration was calm and capable, and the teaching faculty skilled and knowing.

I had suffered initiation into puberty and a coming-of-age consciousness in the company of thirty kids in a small schoolhouse that remained largely unchanged for four years. The gigantic Arlington - with its hordes of swaggering upper classmen and lockers and beautiful, disdainful girls and chemistry labs and letter-festooned, chiseled athletes - absolutely terrified me. I felt like I'd been swimming about in a tiny, comfortable aquarium that had suddenly been dumped into a seething ocean. There were predators and threatening shadows and dangers aplenty, and my old chums were now spread far and wide. Many of them seemed to blend into the new population with ease, while I hung back and grew more isolated.

There was one exception. In freshman orientation class I was seated next to a big red-haired kid with a huge cast on one leg.

"Broke it playing football," John explained as he propped his crutches against the wall.

"Oh," I replied. I'd never played football, let alone done something so glorious as fracture a limb. I was ready to withdraw from the exchange; but John, son of a Lutheran pastor and in possession of one of the most effusive personalities I'd ever encountered, wouldn't let it go.

"Do you like music?" he demanded happily.

"Yes," I admitted, miserable.

"What do you like?" he pressed.

My grudging answer began a friendship that would last for decades. We discovered that we both enjoyed the same bands and styles, and soon we were spending long hours in his basement listening to endless stacks of albums. He had a *lot* of records. We both played guitar and sang, and soon we were joining bands together, creating and recording our own tunes.

John was unique in many ways; in fact, to this very day, I'd say he may be the most unique person I've ever met. He was brilliant and quick and funny and passionate, a force of nature that would not be denied.

And he was also the very first person of my generation I'd ever gotten to know who was pro-actively anti-racist.

Everyone - and I mean without exception – seemed racist to one degree or another. Some were overtly and loudly so, while others were more passive in their bigotry. But all my peers seemed universally racist. *All of them.* Except John. He was the first of my friends to openly espouse the radical notion that alienation and antipathy between blacks and whites wasn't part of the natural order, and he could become quite exercised about it.

He came from a long line of theologically-inclined intellectuals and educated individuals (one of his ancestors had been a judge in the Salem witch trials, and his paternal grandfather had a building named after him on Ohio's Wittenberg University campus), and he would permit no bigoted banter among our friends. Any racist comment would be met with unbridled scorn from John, who would instantly and vigorously upbraid the person uttering it. John stood six-feet-four and weighed two hundred and fifteen pounds, and he was loud and unmistakable in his intent to ban racist language and attitudes in his presence.

He was one of the first of us to get a driver's license, and soon he was driving everybody around. One afternoon, as we were on our way to a band practice, our drummer leaned out the window and yelled

"Nigger!" at some black guy walking down the sidewalk.

John went into paroxysms behind the wheel. I was certain that if his wrecking didn't kill the drummer (and the rest of us), then he would most certainly do it with his bare hands. That kid, the drummer, never made that mistake again.

His attitude simultaneously perplexed, intrigued, and inspired me. Knowing him caused me to look at my own attitudes for the very first time, and I began to wonder if the sense of racial superiority I'd known from childhood might be misplaced. Arlington was a microcosm of the shifting racial attitudes in our country: its population had also shifted markedly to the black side of the spectrum as white flight continued and neighborhoods changed. There were interracial fights and brawls, and on a couple of occasions the school had to be closed because of racially-ignited clashes…not riots exactly, but perhaps something close.

John was an energetic defender of enforced busing, the mandatory mixing of black and white students by transporting kids across school district lines.

"It forces us to be together, to get to know each other," he explained. It was a hot-button issue in our city and elsewhere, but he was right. Even at School 1, I hadn't really interacted with the black kids, but at Arlington I did.

It turned out that I had a talent for writing and making speeches, two of the focal points my grade school's gifted program focused on. When I was a sophomore I entered the Optimist Oratorical Contest, a public speaking competition sponsored by the philanthropic Optimists International. I made it through a few preliminary bouts and ended up in the state finals. The Optimists put the finalists up in a downtown hotel for the judging, and I ended up rooming with Chas. Chas was black.

Chas was hilarious and we quickly grew close: we spent the entire weekend at each other's side, and my parents were amused at my new friend's color. On Friday night the chaperones took us all to see Norman Jewison's *In the Heat of the Night*, a film about a black cop from Philadelphia who becomes involved in a murder investigation in Mississippi. The irony didn't escape Chas or me, but our conversations afterward never went to the racial themes of the movie. It didn't matter. We were just two kids away from our parents for a weekend having fun.

Chas won the state contest. I finished in the Top 10, and we maintained contact for a while. And then, as it often goes with long-distance friendships, we simply stopped communicating. But he was my first. My first black friend.

There were others, but not many.

Jerry was an amazing sight- bushy afro, tinted granny glasses, fatigue jacket, and one black glove worn like those worn by Tommie Smith and John Carlos at the 1968 Olympics medal ceremony. It all came together to form a striking and formidable image. I found him so cool-looking and so terrifying all at the same time. The white kids at school knew he was trouble, but beyond that we knew nothing about him at all. If a student dustup had racial overtones, you could depend on Jerry being implicated.

He was the very embodiment of what whites seemed to fear most and he was unapologetically overt in his blackness. He was a couple of years younger, and I don't think we ever exchanged more than a couple of brief glances in the hallway. Mostly we moved in wholly separate circles...until a guy in his class, a white kid I knew from music connections, approached me with an idea.

Every spring the school held a talent show, and tryouts were coming up. Acts auditioned before a panel of teachers and students, and my white friend assured me that if we teamed up with Jerry and his brother Bobby, we'd be a shoo-in. He reasoned that, given the racial atmosphere and the ubiquitous calls from student leaders and faculty for reconciliation, a black-white act couldn't fail to make the cut.

I'd already made a reputation for being a decent guitarist and I knew my friend to be a competent bass player. Jerry apparently sang and his younger brother played drums. And since they were *black*, I assumed they'd be good. There seemed to be no way we'd fail, so I agreed to sit in. Within a week I found myself in the home of a black person for the first time. Ever.

We set up in their oldest brother's basement and worked up a couple of tunes, Buddy Miles' *Them Changes* and *Groove Me* by King Floyd. Bobby played with a classic "parade grip" and started every tune with "One, two, ready, play." Jerry sang decently and his brother was solid on the drums. My friend and I did our parts competently as their backup men, and one afternoon we carried our gear over to Arlington's auditorium and played for the judges. When the results were posted a day or two later, we didn't make the cut.

I was shocked. I *know* we played well enough, and I made it into the show with another act, all white. For the first and only time in my life, I genuinely believed I was the victim of racial discrimination. I think Jerry's shamelessly brandished single black glove kept the judges from even hearing us. As far as they were concerned, he was a troublemaker…a *black* troublemaker, and our whiteness couldn't mask his in-your-face pride. Or maybe we sucked. But I doubt it. We were good, dammit.

The band didn't stay together, and I'm not sure I ever talked with either of the brothers again. There were no hard feelings, nothing like that. In truth, other than to discuss how the music should be played, we didn't talk much at all, let alone enter a deep dialogue about race relations. After the brief intersection of our two worlds, we went our separate ways. Jerry orchestrated a few more protests, I reported on them for the paper, and the school was even locked down a time or two because of race fights.

I graduated from high school and entered Indiana University's regional campus in Indianapolis on a pre-med tract, though that soon gave way to a double-major in philosophy and psychology and with a religion minor. I heard several years later that Jerry died, but I have no idea if that's true or not. What I *do* know is that, as I entered undergraduate life in a major metropolitan school, I fully understood that the bigoted worldview I'd inherited from three centuries of family tradition was terribly and tragically flawed.

I want to end this chapter with describing as best I can what I take my current disposition to be, and I'm going to borrow several pages from the playbook of the 12 Step movement...from Alcoholics Anonymous, Narcotics Anonymous, and such. I am more than passingly familiar with their ideas.

I am a racist and I always will be. I can't help it, any more than an alcoholic can ever *not* be an alcoholic. In the view of 12 Step culture, alcoholism can never be cured, but it can be admitted, faced, dealt with, and controlled: the alcoholic, if he is willing to admit the insidious and pervasive nature of his disease, can *transcend* his alcoholism. In that sense, I think I can genuinely describe myself as a "recovering" racist.

I can do nothing about the way I was brought up. Racial prejudice was as much a part of my reality growing up as north was north and west was west. Despite that, I have learned that I can rise above my bequeathed bigotry, just as an addict can rise above his addiction. The human project, at the level of the individual, is the willful and determined transcending of the given destructive elements of his biography. To invoke an old image, while we may have no control over the cards we're dealt, we most certainly have a great deal of control over how we play them. If I can recognize and acknowledge my racism for what it is, then I can by conscious means deny its hold on me. Each day, I can choose not to act out on my bigotry.

Any 12 Stepper with a long claim to sobriety will tell you that eventually his not drinking becomes a matter of habit, which isn't to say that the inclination - the desire to indulge - disappears. It doesn't. That drive to drink may raise its ugly head during times of stress; oddly, for some of us, it's most likely to appear when things are going well. I personally am most tempted when everything seems to be going my way. I call it the "Let's celebrate!" dynamic. But even in those times, I've learned how to back up and examine my inclinations and – at least, so far – choose another option, the option not to take a drink or swallow a pill. Not right now. Not today.

Similarly, I may find myself in situations that conjure my youthful bigotry; maybe I get cut off in traffic, or maybe I'm in the jury pool, and the defendant involved is black. The racist feelings might begin to bubble up like some old toothache, but then I remind myself to recognize them for what they are – corrosive, damaging, and born of meaningless hatred and fear – and seize them and cast them back into the pit...until the next time. I'll return to this notion later.

My mother lived to be 93 years old. One February she fell in the apartment where she'd lived independently. While the incident itself didn't cause any injuries, the stress of it set in motion a process that led to her decline over the next several weeks. She died on April 1.

I had occasion to visit with her numerous times during this last period, and sometimes our conversations would venture out of the safety of day-to-day small talk. She once puzzled over why she had lived so long. She'd watched dozens of friends and loved ones pass away, leaving her behind. Alone. She didn't understand it; she almost seemed resentful of her longevity.

"God must have something left for me to do," she reasoned.

"Maybe so," I returned lamely. I really had no desire to attempt to uncover what the Master of the Universe's agenda might be and steered the talk elsewhere.

Nearer the end, our conversations became more and more sparse. One day, as she lay on her bed emaciated, wrapped in a diaper, and growing visibly wearier, she spoke up, à propos of nothing I could see.

"I'm not prejudiced anymore," she said flatly.

"What's that?" I asked, leaning in from my chair.

"I'm not prejudiced anymore," she repeated.

And thinking this was indeed a remarkable late-in-the-game development, I asked, "How so?"

"They're all so nice to me here," she said.

"Who?"

"The black people. They really seem to care about me."

I settled back in my chair, a thin wry smile on my lips. Maybe, I reflected with dark humor, God had been able to check something off his eternal to-do list after all.

Along with my mother, none of my relatives seem to exhibit any overt racist behavior anymore, although something one of my older cousins said recently caused me to wonder. I have no idea where any of them are with it. We don't talk about it.

What I do know is that all of us sprung from the same corrupt soil of racism, and it infused every fiber of our beings with its poison. It still resides there, and how they deal it is unknown to me. It resides there because of three hundred years of overt bigotry, beginning with the very first of our ancestors to land on these American shores. Every new generation passed it on to the next, and in the next chapter I want to tell you three stories, not necessarily related, that helped to define the racist climate in which I was raised. I first heard these stories, in one fashion or another, from my mother. While she didn't have many details, it turns out she related them more-or-less accurately. I've been bequeathed a set of ancient skeletons possessing most of their bones, and I want to outfit them with flesh as best I can. But remember, this is ultimately *my* story, the narrative of my journey. Even if, as I occasionally determined, the tales I heard weren't entirely historically accurate, they still served to help form my racial consciousness. And maybe the old stories might somehow hold the key to my own evolution. Perhaps. We'll see.

If the sins of the fathers are visited on the sons, then maybe the sons can eventually expunge that same guilt.

Chapter 2

A Soul Freed?

None of us prosecutes our lives in isolation. We all conduct our journeys in context, a context that eventually may be mapped and examined. At that point, in retrospect, we often see the route more clearly, how we scaled certain heights and avoided others, where we swam in foaming oceans and waded in tranquil brooks, how we survived parched deserts and thrived in lush forests. We're able to review the long roster of traveling companions, those who departed too quickly and those who remained, those we miss and those whom we hope to never see again.

And ideally, if enough wisdom has accrued along the way, we'll be able to sort out those elements that imparted life to us and those that were toxic; we will be able to differentiate the chaff from the wheat. It's from that older-and-hopefully-wiser perspective that I initially intended to offer three stories from my family's annals, but on further reflection, in order to not upset the rhythm of my primary narrative, I've decided to assign two of the anecdotes to the appendix. After all, they only relate to each other in that they were first told to me by my mother, and each of them seized my imagination in one way or another. The final one, though, is my reason for writing in the first place. It has haunted me for a long time, but it may provide the greatest promise of healing for my festering racist wound.

I would encourage you to read the two at the back of the book since they provide insight into understanding how my family's history is woven into the broader racist fabric of this nation. And, frankly, they're pretty interesting.

There is an area on the western shore of Ireland that runs through Counties Galway and Mayo known as Joyce country. It's a gorgeous, rolling, green place and many of the folk there still speak Gaelic as their primary tongue. The first time I saw it I literally felt as if I had at long last returned home, even though I'd never stepped foot on its rocky soil before. The smell of acrid burnt peat hung seamlessly in the air, small bands of sheep with rainbow colors painted across their backs meandered carelessly in front of our car, the ceaseless breeze off the sea caressed us gently. One particularly blustery afternoon I knelt before my wife of thirty years on a high cliff looking out over the thrashing Atlantic and asked her, once again, to marry me. Luckily, she accepted, and I presented her with an emerald-set Claddagh ring, a piece of jewelry originally designed by one of my ancestors* and bought for its intended purpose. That evening a priest friend renewed our vows under the low smoky ceiling of a centuries-old pub.

The Joyces were one of the "Twelve Tribes" of Galway, merchant families of Norman origin who dominated Galway's political and commercial life for generations. The Bay of Galway has long hosted seafaring vessels from Europe, and the Twelve Tribes oversaw and controlled that sea trade, making out very well in the process. Henry Joyce was the mayor in Galway in the mid-16th century, and one can only surmise that my Irish ancestors were well-to-do during his administration.

But all things must come to an end, and in the rebellion against England a mere century later, the Twelve Tribes sided with the Irish Catholics, fearing inevitable repression should the Cromwellian protestants win; they did, and after a particularly brutal campaign led by Cromwell himself, Galway was besieged and conquered. Cromwell's army, under the authority of the English Parliament, confiscated the Tribes' property and disenfranchised their members.**

*Tradition has it that Richard Joyce, a Galway silversmith around 1700, was kidnapped by pirates en route to the West Indies, where, pining for his beloved, he designed the ring. Ransomed after several years in captivity, he returned home and gave the ring to his sweetheart and married her. The ring has been consistently produced in Joyce country since.

**In one of those great ironies of family history, one of my father's ancestors fought *with* Cromwell in hope of advancing Presbyterianism. After the "New Model Army's" victory, he was rewarded with land. I have no idea where, but probably in Ulster.

The Tribes eventually came to form a kind of middle class under the new regime and gain a tolerable, if not opulent, lifestyle. However, after the Jacobite defeat at the end of the 17th century, they lost any remaining power, influence, and – to a large degree –prosperity. It was from this downtrodden posture of defeat that someone named Alexander Joyce, sometime around 1720, probably came to America.

I have no notion of how old Alexander was when he left Ireland; I have no notion what his financial state was. I don't know if he departed destitute or if he managed to secret away a grubstake. I do know that after landing somewhere in Virginia (at least according to my family tradition) with his two sons, Alexander and Thomas, he eventually made good: almost sixty years later, in his will of 1778 filed in North Carolina, he parcels out more than 1200 acres of land, numerous horses, and pounds and pounds of money to a dozen children. He also bequeaths to his heirs eighteen slaves.

Alexander identifies the slaves - the "negroes" – by name: Ned, Sue, Pegg (sic) and her two unnamed children, Dick, Jenny, Will, Hagar, Caesar, Jude, Sam, Nan, Amy, Dinah, another Jenny, Jacob, and Agnis (sic). Sometimes he appears to keep families together, sometimes not. Alexander's son, Andrew, in addition to receiving two hundred acres and one hundred pounds, is left "one negroe (sic) boy named Sam." Sam must've been someone's child, and we don't know his age, but clearly he didn't remain with his birth family.

Undeniably, regardless of the condition in which he arrived, Alexander prospered in his new home, a prosperity that just as undeniably was built on the backs of the black slaves he harbored. Since they were regarded as property, it wasn't unusual for slaves to appear as bequests in the wills of the period. Something that *is* unusual is the fact that, in Alexander's will, the only one of his children not to be given a slave is Thomas. Why? There's no way of knowing.

Curiously, Thomas' only inheritance is ten pounds of money...no slaves, no property, no horses. And the amount of money is paltry compared to the sums left to his siblings. Again, we don't know why, but there may be clues. Alexander, as part of the bequest to Thomas, also leaves far more, one hundred pounds, to Thomas' son Joseph. And Thomas himself files a will only two years later than his father, in 1780.

I can only speculate as to why Thomas' annotated inheritance was so sparse. With my 21st century sensibilities I'm tempted to fantasize that perhaps he was of an anti-slavery disposition, but his own will quickly puts the lie to that: he assigns sixteen slaves by name to his own children, and we'll return to that in a moment. It's far more likely that, as the oldest surviving son (his brother, the junior Alexander, passed away shortly before his father), he was already a well-established and endowed plantationer himself. A bequest any larger would've represented a serious slight to his siblings. In fact, wills were typically only written when the subject had specific bequests to make; otherwise, the ancient practice of *primogeniture* prevailed, and the oldest male inherited all the land. Alexander's will really wasn't for Thomas at all; it's for his siblings…his male siblings. Women rarely were gifted with land, and in fact Alexander only "lends" 240 acres to his surviving wife Jane. On her death, it was to become the permanent property of his son Robert.

The slaves he assigns her, Ned, Sue, and Pegg and her two small children, are also only "lent." With chilling detachment Alexander requests that, on his wife's death, the five slaves on loan to her, as well as any of their "increase," are to be sold and the money arising from this sale be "equally divided amongst all my sons which shall at that time be living." There's no request that spouses be kept together or that children should stay with their parents, no more than there might've been for a foal to have been kept with a mare.

Lethal disease in those times was common to a degree that we can't even comprehend. Death was the looming guest at every gathering, every church service, every family dinner; death was the unwelcome midwife at every birth. Thomas, Alexander's second son, begins his will by saying that he is "sick, but of disposing mind and memory." He may have dictated it from his deathbed, as was often the case. And to be sure, he, his father, and his older brother all died within two years of one another.

Thomas did well for himself, too. His will names ten children to whom he distributes vast acreage, money, horses, furniture, and sixteen slaves. Unlike his father's, Thomas' will outlines certain formulae and even provisos for his bequests: if John doesn't equally divide the land on which he resides with his brother George, then John must forego title to two slaves, Peter and Amy. He also warns George that he has six years to "reform from vicious courses and take a prudent care for a living," or he forfeits his inheritance altogether. George, apparently, had issues.

That the father should impose conditions on his bequests isn't particularly surprising: fathers and sons have had falling outs for millennia, and sometimes fathers have insisted on having their way even at the end. While I wish I knew why Thomas accused George of "vicious courses," I'm certain George knew what he meant. I, however, never will. The next generation's dynamics become more intriguing to me still.

Thomas' firstborn son, yet another Alexander and referred to in my family's archives as "Alexander I," seems to have fared well, too. But in his bequests, his resources have become more scant than his father's or grandfather's: his children are left far smaller parcels of land, and the cash amounts are expressed in shillings rather than pounds. Only four slaves are assigned, all to be "lent" to his widow until her passing; then they were to go to his sons. To his son William he gives Phillis and her child Lucy; to John, a boy named

Charles; and to his firstborn, known in the archives as Alexander II, he presents a boy named Price.

Price. When I first saw his name in my ancestor's will I felt a chill run up my spine. This was the very slave I'd heard about in my mother's stories when I was a child, the freeman whose resting place I'd determined to find so long ago. His mention in my ancestor's last will and testament, the ancient Alexander who had first made his way to Indiana and for whom my own son was named, came to me like the soft whispering voice of an old friend. Somehow, I felt strongly drawn to this man who, according to my mother, loved his master so much that, despite having been freed, he chose to stay with him as a family member and move to a new and dangerous land. This was Price, *our* Price. Seeing his name in Alexander II's will made me more resolute than ever to find him.

I had no idea what finding Price would mean to me; I really never understood why I cared so much. I just knew it was important, that it was something I needed to do. I only slowly came to understand that it was ultimately about atonement.

Remember, I think of myself as a recovering racist. Just as an alcoholic can never truly be cured of his addiction, I've come to understand that racism is part of my very constitution. Because I was steeped in it for so long and at so young an age, I know that its poison reaches through every aspect of my psyche. My personal project is to recognize it for the irrational contaminant that it is and pursue better ends despite it. I now know that finding Price has been my way of personally making amends for my racism; he's my *direct* connection to my ancestors' dark history and my coming to terms with it. Simply put, I understand that I needed to find Price in order to apologize, an apology that I know can never be adequate: there is no manner of apology that will ever be equal to such horrendous, systemic evil. But I was determined to try, and then honestly and humbly share the story with anyone who wished to hear it.

My mother had told me that Alexander left Virginia angry with his father for being slighted in the will, and that he had taken "his mule and his nigger" and headed west for St. Louis to make a new life for himself. In her telling of it, they – Alexander, the mule, and Price - never made it, getting only as far as Indiana. There they stayed, and there, five generations later, I was born.

Mom didn't have her story quite right on a number if counts, as it turns out. I'm pretty certain she was faithfully passing on what she had been told by her father, since I have a manuscript from my aunt that recounts the same gabled narrative. It only seems reasonable that my mother and her sister would've been told the same tale originally, and the teller of that tale was probably my grandfather, Alexander's great-grandson. But my grandfather had some of his facts wrong, and some simply conflated with others. As I looked more deeply into the oldest accounts, I discovered a fascinating tale that painted a far different picture than the one I'd been told.

The fundamental question for me is, why did Alexander leave Virginia in the first place? In his will of 1817, his father leaves him two hundred acres, a mill, a "sorrel mare," and "one negro boy named Price." Clearly Alexander was a propertied man, so why did he leave his home?

His reasons were probably not so different as anyone's might be- financial, family conflict, political leanings, wanderlust…maybe all the above. And frankly, we'll probably never know. However, clues lurk in the old family documents and in American history.

There's a learning curve to everything, including the macroeconomics of a burgeoning nation. The Panic of 1819 is considered to be our country's first great economic cataclysm, brought on largely by fiscal irresponsibility at the highest levels…as it almost always is.

Our worst decisions tend to be made not only in panic, but in euphoria as well. Thirty years ago, after the birth of my son, I was put on a steady diet of antidepressants and anti-anxiety drugs after I'd suffered a complete mental collapse requiring a hospital stay. I recovered, but because my usual inhibitions and emotional restraints were compromised by the prescription meds,

I made some financial decisions during that period that nearly bankrupted my family. This was about the time Federal Reserve Chairman Alan Greenspan noted the "irrational exuberance" prevailing in the financial markets during the dot-com rave of the '90's was unfounded optimism in the future of technology.* And he was right. When the bubble burst at the turn of the millennium, billions of dollars and thousands of jobs were lost, and investments simply evaporated overnight into the foundationless mist they'd been created from.

And so it has ever been. When our view of the present, and more significantly, the future, becomes unreasonably skewed to the positive, we tend to make financial decisions that, from a broader, more temperate perspective, are unwise. In our giddiness we believe we somehow have less to lose; but there's always plenty to lose. There's *everything* to lose.

The American victory over the British in the War of 1812 was followed by a period of such giddiness on a national level. After the Revolutionary War, England hadn't relinquished the colonies happily, and it maintained a kind of cold war with the nascent United States, particularly on the sea and in trade. Some historians see this war as a late expression of the Napoleonic conflicts, and some view it as the American

*In his 1993 book, *Listening to Prozac,* psychiatrist Peter Kramer even suggested that the tech boom was being fueled by the wide prescribing of anti-depressants, leading less emotionally inhibited investors to dump money into companies they might've otherwise avoided.

Revolution, Part 2. I tend to see it more as the latter: British sailors kidnapped Americans at sea and forced them into service, and England entered into secret trade pacts with other countries that undercut American efforts. We rightfully took these as major affronts and declared war on the greatest naval power in the world. Understandably, it didn't go particularly well for us…at first.

After a couple of years of British supremacy, which included the burning of Washington DC and Indian-assisted skirmishes throughout the Northwest territories, the Americans' sea-going cut-and-run guerilla war eventually began to turn things in our favor. England was fabulously over-extended in its dealings with Napoleon in Europe and mandated increasingly onerous taxation to fund its wars. Public dissatisfaction at home, combined with a newfound patriotism and enthusiasm for dealing with the unfinished business of the revolution on the part of the Americans (Francis Scott Key wrote the lyrics for *The Star-Spangled Banner* while watching the British bombardment of Boston harbor), eventually led England to peace negotiations at the invitation of President Madison. In what is perhaps the greatest example in history of a "Let's pretend this never happened" ploy, the Treaty of Ghent, signed on Christmas Eve in 1814, essentially put everything back the way it was before the war with little resolved at all. There were vague promises to address the major grievances of the parties later, but by-and-large they were forgotten.

And in another quirk of history, the most spectacular American victory of the war was won by Andrew Jackson and a heavily outnumbered contingent of partisans at New Orleans almost two weeks *after* the treaty was signed. News of the agreement in Ghent and the victory in New Orleans reached the American public at about the same time and were conflated into the general notion that the war had ended with America the victor. However, we most decidedly were not. At best, the War of 1812 ended in a great draw, and many historians argue that we actually lost. But no matter: truth is always in the eye of the beholder.

The period immediately following the war was a time of ebullient afterglow, "The Era of Good Feelings." Political bickering in the government dropped to an all-time low, and just as I had done after my son's birth while all drugged-up, some very poor financial decisions were made, both on the part of state and local governments and on the part of individuals. Self-confidence skyrocketed; risky ventures abounded. Loans were sought and granted that never should have been, all because everyone felt like winners.

But, as any pair of lovers will tell you, afterglow only lasts so long. Eventually the snipping and sniping begins again, and sometimes with a vengeance.

The Second Bank of the United States wasn't actually a government entity, but part of its chartered task was to control the currency in the country, much as the Federal

Reserve does now. It was established after the "victorious" War of 1812 and its governors were made up of eastern overseers. Already harboring inherent suspicions of westerners and southerners, these governors began to get cold feet when they saw how over-extended and lax credit had become after the war. They began to call in loans and thus began – from the top down – a cycle that would eventually leave vast numbers of Americans penniless.

The Panic of 1819 may not have been entirely due to the Second Bank's actions (the economic structure of a nation is never entirely the burden of any one institution, regardless of how "too big to fail" it might be), but they certainly exacerbated it. The bank would call in a loan, and the party having taken out that loan would then have to call in subsequent debts or liquidate assets in order to pay the bank, and so on and so on, until there was no one left to buy the assets and no assets to sell. A general economic panic set in nationwide, and perhaps my ancestor, Alexander II, was caught up in the stampede.

Again, according to family records, on his father's death in 1818, Alexander received two hundred acres of land in Patrick County, Virginia, with a working mill on it. He also was bequeathed a horse, and of course, the slave boy, Price.

Maybe, in the recession following the Panic, Alexander's position became so compromised that he was forced to sell his property and mill; and, again, I had no clue what type of mill it night have been…lumber, grist, whatever. Maybe he freed Price because he couldn't maintain him; in family lore we're told the emancipated young man remained with the family because he was so "devoted" to them. It sounds cozy and amenable, even noble.

In any case, the family history, compiled by my great-aunt Flora, says that sometime in the 1820s, Alexander sold the land and the mill, built two flat boats to carry wagons loaded with household goods, and took eight horses to begin navigating a swollen tributary of the Ohio River north. Alexander's goal, according to my aunt, was to reach a slavery-free state, because accompanying him, along with his sons, was his single freed slave, Price. One account names Kansas as the intended destination; another names St. Louis. But if Alexander was seeking a free state, neither purported endpoint makes sense: Missouri was very much a slave state, and Kansas wasn't a state at all. It wasn't admitted to the union until 1861 in the buildup to the Civil War. It came in as a free state but prior to that it represented a kind of line-in-the-sand where both pro- and anti-slavery coalitions had faced off. Unless Alexander had some other compelling reason to head for Kansas - perhaps a business opportunity - it just wouldn't have been the best choice, considering Price. And Missouri most certainly was not.

When Alexander and his party reached Jefferson County in southern Indiana, the river became impassable because of ice. They decided to pass the winter there, intending to set out again in spring; but they didn't. They remained in Madison for a couple of years, and the family appears in the federal census of 1830.

But curiously, Price isn't anywhere in the records. Viewing this census was my first clue that Price's story might be a little more complicated than I thought.

I've described how Price's tale had somehow always fascinated me. From my very first hearing of it, I wanted to know more, and I told my mother that I'd like to see his grave. She promised to take me to the tiny family cemetery "someday," and that day arrived when I was maybe fourteen years old. One summer morning Mom packed a picnic lunch and we set out in her copper-colored Mercury station wagon and drove to Acton, the tiny hamlet in southeastern Marion County where I'd been born. My grandmother still lived there. Acton was an old, old settlement: Marion County, the home of the state capitol, Indianapolis, had been opened to settlers in 1822, six short years after Indiana had been admitted to the union. Little Acton's main claim to fame was the presence of more churches (all Protestant) per capita than any other town in Indiana. It was also home to one of eleven "pioneer" cemeteries in the county, our family plot.

Mom wasn't sure where the cemetery was because she hadn't seen it in decades. She had a vague idea; she knew it was located somewhere on the old family homestead, which originally spanned both southern Marion and northern Johnson counties. The two-story brick farmhouse she'd known as a child was there, now rented to strangers; the remainder of the property had been carved up into single-family lots infested by insipid ranch houses. We drove past them until the road became raucous gravel, and then it simply stopped, blocked by a rusted wire livestock fence. We got out of the car and searched through the surrounding woods but found no gravesites. We sat in the car and ate the sandwiches she'd made in silent disappointment.

"I know it was by the creek," she mused, pointing into the woods. "And it's right over there." She shook her head, mystified. But she was wrong. The tiny cemetery wasn't by any creek at all.

Relying on memory, especially family recollections that span generations, is a risky enterprise: it just isn't that reliable. Our search for the cemetery was abandoned for years as adolescence struck and I became distracted by other interests. But I never forgot about it, never forgot about Alexander and his exodus from Virginia, and I most certainly never forgot about Price. Life occurred: college, marriage, career, children. I was in my mid-forties before we reconvened the quest, and this time we were better prepared.

My father had died and mom had remarried. She and my stepfather were visiting from their home in southern Florida when she decided to make some phone calls to old friends about the graveyard, and they quickly paid off. It turned out that the dead-end dirt road hadn't always been so: originally it had continued through the fields, eventually leading to the cemetery. Now the little graveyard was surrounded by a big commercial property owned by a business distributing enormous tanks of propane gas; its office was in a military-like Quonset hut sitting in a bleak gravel lot. And just beyond it was the graveyard. On a hot August morning in 1997, my wife and I, our nine-year-old son (the ancient Alexander's namesake) and my mother and stepfather finally found it.

It had suffered from decades of neglect, barely recognizable. We found a tragic mess, including an intermittently corroded wire fence featured a mockery of a gate, permanently rusted open. The grass inside the fence was almost waist-high, but we saw occasional sparse spots that we discovered to be rude oases where grave markers lay flat on the ground.

My son and I tugged at a few of them, and I struggled to make out the inscriptions- King, Rubush, Joyce, all related family surnames from the mid-19th century. Without doubt we were in the right place, and we knew for certain when we discovered the unkempt headstone featured in the next photograph; it belonged to Mary Elizabeth, Alexander's wife. We found a number of other names we recognized, but not the one I most eagerly sought. We left disappointed. My mother and stepfather took dozens of chigger bites with them as souvenirs; Peg, Jess, and I received none.

Again, years passed. In the spring of 2014 my mother died, having only recently informed me she was no longer a racist. She passed on April Fools' Day, her final prank. I became the custodian of her family archives, and they were substantial: photographs, letters, documents, newspaper and magazine articles- all neatly organized, labeled, and catalogued. I sealed the big boxes and put them in the back of my closet. I opened them two years later and discovered an absolute treasure trove.

She'd made it easy. My mother was many things, but above all she was organized. The pictures and papers were arranged in neat groups by families and time frames. I found pictures of my grandfather, who, when young, looked strikingly like my son; my grandmother was a gorgeous template of my daughter. I found love letters she'd received from my grandfather and pictures of his general store. There was the original deed with Andrew Jackson's signature for Alexander II's eighty acres in Indiana, and it all made me recall the little cemetery and my failed search for Price's grave. I decided to visit it once again, and I determined to restore the dilapidated graveyard to its rightful condition.

Unlike me, my wife has a prodigious sense of direction.
She led me to the plot, past the houses and Quonset hut,
straight to the gate. I was amazed to see the gate and
fence had been restored. The grass was neat and
clipped short, and the headstones were upright in neat
lines. A number of the original foot stones were there
as well, and I later learned that they had been key in
locating the graves: unlike headstones, they rarely

become dislocated. There looked to be eleven markers, but once again, none showing Price.

The first thing that occurred to me was that perhaps the family history had again been mistaken, and he'd been interred under a different name. I checked the publicly available cemetery records against the headstones and our genealogy: other than Price, all were present and accounted for. I was doubly perplexed; first, that the cemetery had been mysteriously restored, and second, even in its current pristine shape, Price's grave remained unmarked. I became determined more than ever to find him, first by discovering who had restored the plot.

Aunt Flora's documents on Alexander II had originally been assembled and published by the Franklin Township Historical Society. They'd also published an article or two by my mother, so I felt comfortable visiting them in the abandoned church they had converted to a small museum. They had no idea who had restored the cemetery but pointed me to the larger Marion County Genealogical Society, which was headquartered in Washington Park Cemetery on the far eastside of Indianapolis. There I learned that all of the "pioneer cemeteries" in the county were maintained by the trustee of the township in which they were located. The Franklin Township trustee had contracted with a firm that restored and maintained cemeteries. Mystery solved. But no one – neither the historical societies nor the trustee – had any record of Price's burial. So far, no *official* documentation indicated Price had ever existed outside of our old family stories and Aunt Flora's unsubstantiated history.

I had to admit that it was possible that Price had never made it to Indiana. He was mentioned in his father's will as being left to Alexander II in Virginia, but after that, nothing. He isn't mentioned in the Jefferson County census of 1830, he isn't mentioned among the Joyce family in the Marion County census of 1840, he isn't listed in any of the numerous burial records documenting the interments of the cemetery, and he had no gravestone. He just evaporates from the historical record.

But I just wasn't content to leave it at that, and this is where the story takes a bit of an eerie twist.

For the past forty years or so I've earned my living as a remodeling contractor. I consider the title pejorative, pretty much synonymous with "thief." Whenever asked for my occupation, I always respond "carpenter," since that's a proper honorific for a craftsman; still, it doesn't really encompass all I do.

Many years ago I was preparing to put in the foundation for a residential room addition when the homeowner warned me that he had buried an underground electrical line in a plastic pipe connecting his house to a distant barn. He was fairly certain it crossed right through the footprint of our proposed dig, but he assured me he could show me where it was. The excavator was already on-site and on the clock, but I was hesitant to take the man's word for it: a mistake of only a few inches could be disastrous.

"Here, I'll show you," he chirped, disappearing into his house. He returned a few minutes later with two coat hangers and a pair of wire cutters. He cut two sections out of the hangers about twelve inches long, then bent them both at right angles. He held each of them in his hands loosely pointing away from his chest, then began pacing back and forth over the area where he believed the buried conduit to be. Consistently, as he moved over one certain spot, the wires would swing in toward each other, crossing. As he moved away from the spot, the wires would relax back into their original positions.

As my coworkers and I watched, he worked his way from the house to the barn, the wires crossing to detail a gentle sweeping curve connecting the buildings.

"That's it," he smiled. "Pretty much as I recall it."

"Give me those," I scoffed, taking the wires. Mimicking him, I began crisscrossing the same area and in complete bewilderment felt the wires cross *by themselves* along the same lines he'd walked.

He laughed. "Some people can do it, some can't. My father could, and I can. Looks like you can, too."

I repeated the process a few times to convince myself, handing the wires to my helper. They didn't work for him. I grabbed a shovel and began gingerly turning the earth where the wires had indicated, and within a few minutes exposed the white PVC pipe. He gave me the bent coat hangers in reward and I have them today. I've used them numerous times on various jobsites, always successfully.

I had discovered that I had the ability to "witch," just like the old-timers with their divining rods. Science is mixed and many authorities deny it completely; and others consider it a commonplace phenomenon. No one appears to know why it works, but there seems to be an element of heredity to it. My wife can't do it, nor my son, but my daughter can. In 2016 Peg and I returned to the cemetery, and I had my bent coat hanger wires with me.

At the time, I didn't even know "grave witching" was a thing. I knew I'd been able to locate various things underground with the wires; ironically, the one thing I've never tried to find is water, which is what divining has historically been about. It stood to reason that I'd be able to locate a subterranean disturbance as significant as a grave. Peg opened the cemetery gate as I stood just outside it, wires in position and at the ready.

I understand if you find what happened next unbelievable, but I think you'll have to grant that I've been uncomfortably candid thus far- there's really no reason to start doubting me now. Sadly, we shot no video on this visit, but as I stepped through the gateway, the wires began spinning in opposite directions in 360° circles. I was completely spooked and stopped dead (no pun intended) in my tracks.

I had no idea what to make of the wires' behavior. I'd never seen it before, and I consider myself to be a reasonably rational individual. But this event jarred me out of my willingness to proceed. I dropped the wires immediately and backed out of the cemetery. We left shortly after.

I found myself considering explanations that someone from medieval times would've found satisfying...or maybe a second grader. I was rattled. Shaken. Had I somehow upset spirits standing guard at the cemetery entrance? Had I angered the sleeping souls of my ancestors? I pummeled myself with voodoo theories, my 21st century sensibilities deeply ashamed of the 11th century specters I was conjuring. But there it was: my search for Price was frustrated yet again, and I didn't go back to the cemetery for another year.

By August 2017 I'd regained my composure, although I was still embarrassed by my earlier reaction. Peg and I set out once again, this time planning to record the process. I wasn't going to put the rods in position until I was already inside the gate. As I entered, I made once last concession to my childish concerns from the year before.

"We mean no disrespect," I laughed nervously as I lifted up the wires, holding them chest high, loose in my fingers. I hoped whoever needed to hear my declaration did…whatever that might mean.

We weren't disappointed. As I moved over the line of graves the wires crossed just where they should have. Peg, her phone close, focused on my hands and on how I was supporting the wires in order to assure anyone watching the video that I wasn't doing anything to influence their movement. I think I needed assurance myself, even after all my years of experience.

With every marker we found a grave, one-to-one…no more, no less. I was disappointed and ready to pack it in, but Peg suggested I walk the unmarked areas inside fence. Most of the graves were at the front of the little cemetery, but there was a considerable portion of it that looked unoccupied. I took her suggestion and walked it numerous times, finding nothing.

Until I reached the far corner.

Near a wooden bench that had been placed at the farthest northeast limit of the plot, the rods crossed, then relaxed. They did it three times, in three different spots, but always in the same places as I repeated the process. I seemed to have found three *somethings*. The rods don't indicate what kind of intrusion I find, they only indicate a presence. But judging from the breadth of the indications, it was *possible* that I'd located a grave, or possibly multiple ones. For the first time I thought maybe I'd found Price, the soul that had eluded me for so long.

A few months later, I visited my aunt, my mother's only living sibling, and sorted through mom's memorabilia with a couple of cousins. It was a great afternoon, laughing, crying, remembering. All of us saw and heard things we hadn't before. As I was saying goodbye to my aunt at the end of the day, I mentioned Price and the graveyard. I said nothing about the witching, because, frankly, it's usually easier not to.

"I've been to the cemetery several times now," I said, "but I've never found his grave. I know he's supposed to be buried there."

With an odd look on her face, my aunt replied softly, "Oh, honey, he never had a headstone." I felt a little like the wind had been knocked out of me. Of all the explanations I'd offered myself about why I'd never found him – an assumed name, never having made it to Indiana, never having existed in the first place – the one thing I hadn't considered was that Price lay in an unmarked grave…unacknowledged, unrecognized, unseen. Price the slave, willed to Alexander like a beast, then allegedly freed, only to follow his former master far from his home because he knew nothing else, dead and shoved beneath the ground to be forgotten.

I left my aunt's house amazed at yet another turn in the man's story, and tears came to my eyes more than once on the hour-long drive home. I was outraged for Price, overwhelmed by the disrespect shown to this two-hundred-year-old black man who, so the family story went, had died a Joyce. Before I reached home an idea was beginning to form.

Ron had schooled me more than once. He oversees the Marion County Genealogical Society, the organization I'd visited early in my search. After my witching experience and my aunt's revelation, I went to see him again. I had some troubling questions for him, and he was characteristically accomodating.

"So, he doesn't appear in the census records in either county?" Ron repeated. "Well, he wouldn't," he said flatly. "The Indiana constitution of 1816 – the state's first constitution – made slavery illegal, but the reality was something else altogether."

He went on to explain that of all the states formed from the Northwest Territory, Indiana notoriously turned the blindest eye to the slavery issue. Thousands of slaves were already in Indiana by 1816, serving white masters, so despite the constitution's official rejection of the practice in Article XI, the norm was a don't-ask-don't-tell policy on the part of officials...including white census takers.

"The blacks were just ignored. Even if he was here in 1830, he wouldn't show up in the census," Ron said matter-of-factly.

By 1831 it became almost impossible to even enter the state if you were black, and if you were here you had to have a white-held bond guaranteeing you would never become a drain on public resources. Blacks couldn't own property and couldn't marry, except in extremely unusual circumstances, and they could *never* testify against a white person in a court of law. "Negroes" had virtually no political or civil rights. In short, the only way to exist as a black person in Indiana in the early 19th century was in service to a white man. The family story that Alexander II had freed Price before leaving Virginia was becoming more suspect.

Ron's familiar tone made me risk telling him about the witching in the Joyce cemetery. I guess I shouldn't have been surprised, since he was a man working in an enormous graveyard, but he didn't even wrinkle an eyebrow; he just accepted it unchallenged. I explained that I'd found a promising area in a remote corner of the plot, and he nodded.

"Even today we have 'casual' burials in family plots of individuals who are closely associated but aren't actually relatives. In order to preserve the dignity of the family members – husbands, wives, children – who wanted to be next to one another in the main group, people with less intimate relationships are typically buried farther away.

"And no," he added with grim finality, "he wouldn't have had a marker."

Ron offered one last thought.

"Freeing a slave wasn't an informal affair, you know. Slaves were extremely valuable. It wasn't a matter of just going up to a slave and saying, 'You're free now. Have a nice life.' It was a legal process with plenty of paperwork.

"Any freed slave had to possess a Certificate of Manumission…had to carry it on his person, and if stopped and questioned he'd have to produce it. Otherwise…well, you know."

He shrugged sadly. "It was a lot like transferring titles to a car."

"So," I asked hopefully, "there'd be records? Court records?"

"Should be," Ron said. "In the county where the certificate was issued."

Other than the will of the elder Joyce leaving Price to Alexander II, I had no actual evidence that the man ever existed, and certainly no evidence that he had been freed and willingly accompanied his beloved ex-master to Indiana. Given the history of the times and the idea that Alexander was on his way to Missouri – a slave state – or Kansas – a marginally and *de facto* slave state – I was beginning to suspect Aunt Flora's description of an amicable relationship between Price and Alexander may have been just a well-intentioned fairy tale...maybe one she hadn't originated herself, but a fairy tale nonetheless.

I needed to go to Virginia, Patrick County, where – according to family tradition - Alexander had sold his two hundred acres and mill in order to take his family, his eight horses, his two flat boats, and Price to Indiana. I needed to go to this birthplace of Jeb Stuart, the Confederate general often assigned the responsibility of losing the Battle of Gettysburg. I needed to go to Virginia, my ancestral home, to see if I could find Price.

Chapter 3

Atonement

The events that transpired in Charlottesville, Virginia on the weekend of August 11, 2017 shocked and horrified the nation. In the days that followed, the country was subjected to a torrent of documentaries and news pieces that explicitly depicted the outrageous actions and speech of the rioters and protesters. The public was awakened to the realization that organized Nazis were active in the United States, as well as an "alt-left" who seemed to be equally belligerent. But no event after the tragedy was so gut-wrenching for me as Heather Heyer's funeral and her mother's eulogy.

Susan Bro spoke calmly and with great dignity about her daughter, murdered in the riots, and of her passion for social justice. Her closing words, as I wrestled with the likely treatment of Price in his lifetime, touched me deeply-

> So remember, in your heart, if you're not outraged, you're not paying attention, and I want you to pay attention, find what's wrong, don't ignore it, don't look the other way. Make a point to look at it, and say to yourself, "What can I do to make a difference?"

What *can* I do to make a difference? I wondered. What can *I* do to make a difference? My mind kept returning to the idea that had begun to form after my aunt's revelation that Price's grave had never been marked.

I've called myself a recovering racist, in the sense that racism will always be a permanent element of my biography. My history and the way I was reared is beyond my control but, in the tradition of the 12-Step movement, the way I react to it - the way I prosecute my life in the face of it — is *entirely* under my control.

The 12 Steps of Alcoholics Anonymous is a paradigm of specific strategies for maintaining sobriety in bite-sized chunks, and some of the chunks are more difficult to swallow than others. But this isn't a book about alcoholism; it *is* a book about a kind of recovery, recovery from a racist disposition. Frankly, I think every single human would benefit from working through a 12-Step program of some kind, because I suspect every one of us has a dysfunctional dependence on something...work, food, another person, material possessions, religion. I'm not sure I've ever met an individual who wasn't enslaved to something, and it's certainly not always alcohol or pills.

The 12-Step path involves a process of first acknowledging and owning your dependence, then taking control over it. Several of the steps deal with acknowledging a "greater power," however one chooses to define it. It was pointed out to me long ago that the classic old-man-with-a-long-white-beard isn't the only way to visualize a greater power: the primary consideration is that there are dynamics well beyond us that can contribute to our individual evolution. The salient point is recognizing that the universe doesn't begin and end with *me*. *

Steps 4-7 have to do with acknowledging *specifically* the ways in which our addictions have wreaked damage in our lives, both to ourselves and others, and then making the fully willful decision to turn away from those destructive elements. But it's in working through Steps 8 and 9 that many otherwise well-intentioned and sincere people leave the program.

Why? Because they involve what I'll call atonement, or the attempt to rebalance the equation of destruction that addiction upsets so radically. Step 8 asks us to make a list – an actual list – of everyone we've harmed and be willing to make amends to them. Step 9 is even more terrifying: it calls us to go to those people and make amends – sincerely apologize - except when to do so would result in greater harm.

It's not so difficult to see why so many fold in dealing with steps 8 and 9. Facing someone you've wronged because of your addiction and then humbling yourself enough to seek that person's forgiveness, which of course may never be granted, can be a nauseatingly frightening task. I've made an effort in my adult life to

*I've heard a story about one particularly no-nonsense and grizzled AA member who, after listening to a protracted discussion of this point during a meeting, spoke up in non-negotiable tones. "I call my higher power God," he gruffed, "because that's his fuckin' name."

seek out certain individuals I've wronged, sometimes decades ago, and it's never easy. The person may not even recall the offense. But I do. Approaching them humbly has typically gone far better than I imagined. The spirit of reconciliation is essential in unburdening my soul of the mortal weight of guilt.

I'm not naïve. I understand that there's nothing I can do to make reparation for the sins of my ancestors; our work can only be in the present and it has to be done within the context of our own biographies. But *maybe*, I began to consider in the wake of Charlottesville, I could *symbolically* atone for the past and partly assuage my personal sense of blood-guilt by responding to the call I first heard at my mother's knee from a distant unmarked grave. Maybe Susan Bro's invitation to honor her slain daughter's memory by choosing to make a difference meant honoring Price, a deliberately obscured black man, enslaved and then rendered invisible, obliterated from history almost two centuries ago.

I decided to place a grave marker in the Joyce cemetery for Price. It had been a long time coming, and I wanted to do it properly and legally. I'd learned from Ron at the Marion County Genealogical Society that the little graveyard was presently owned and maintained by the Franklin Township trustee, so I gave that office a call in September 2017. The lady I spoke with there, Debbie, was pleasantly upbeat.

The first thing I asked her was if the cemetery was closed to any further burials. I'd flirted with the idea of requesting that Peg and I be buried there, but she informed me that it wasn't available to any new "occupants." I gingerly asked if a headstone could be added to an existing unmarked grave.

"I guess so," she answered a bit hesitantly. "But we'd need evidence that the person was actually there. Do you have that?"

Now I became quiet, unsure how to proceed. I explained that it had long been a matter of family oral history that Price had accompanied Alexander's family from Virginia, and that he'd been buried in the Joyce cemetery.

"Do you know where the grave is?" Debbie asked.

"I *think* so," I replied.

"You think so?" she repeated. "Is there a depression in the ground or something?"

"No, nothing like that."

"Then why do you think you know where it is?"

"I'm really hesitant to say," I said apologetically. "You're probably going to think it's pretty far-fetched."

"Try me. I've heard about everything."

I cleared my throat. "Have you ever heard of grave witching?"

"Oh, sure!" she said. She sounded like I'd asked her if she'd ever tried lasagna. "That's not so strange. Did someone locate the grave that way?"

"Yeah," I said sheepishly. "Me."

Feeling a little braver, I told her the story of getting three indications in the far corner of the graveyard, and added that such a spot would make sense, given the circumstances.

She was encouraging. "Okay. Put together whatever you have and let us take a look at it. We'll see what we can do." I thanked her and hung up feeling more hopeful than ever.

I had Aunt Flora's published but undocumented account. It had been on file and known to the people in Franklin Township and the Indiana State Library since 1969. It contained the text of Alexander's father's will, bequeathing the two hundred acres, the mill, and Price to his son. And I could argue that Price had gone unmentioned in the 1830 and 1840 Indiana censuses because of conditions in the state at the time. I could advance similar arguments for why his grave wouldn't have been marked, and why his body would've been consigned to the most remote part of the cemetery.

And I had the video of my witching experience; but I wanted more.

I wanted to be able to document Price's freedom, thinking it might make it more plausible that he'd followed Alexander to Indiana, and for that I'd need some record of his manumission through the legal system of Virginia. Ideally I could discover something that would stipulate his existence and his being freed by Alexander, and I hoped I might even locate the old family property with its mill. Maybe I might even learn why they left Virginia in the first place. So, late in March 2018 Peg and I packed her car and left for Patrick County, Virginia, seeking…*something*.

The legend of Brigadoon is about a village in the Scottish highlands that becomes frozen in time; enchanted, it reappears for only one day every one hundred years. On that day it can receive visitors. If an outsider falls in love with one of its inhabitants, he – or presumably she – can remain as a permanent resident.

My business was in Stuart, Virginia, the seat of Patrick County at their genealogical museum. Still, when Peg looked for lodging, she decided she wanted to stay in nearby Floyd, one county to the north. We wound down gauzy county roads, twisting through mountain ridges along white-crested streams, until we finally found the little town of Floyd. We agreed that we had found Brigadoon, but Brigadoon with the attendant cultural dichotomies of the modern south.

Floyd is an anachronism nestled deep among the hills of the Blue Ridge, with the immaculately maintained parkway of the same name running along its southern extreme. It has a population of only a few hundred permanent residents, many of whom seem to be hippie holdovers. The owner of the bed-and-breakfast where we stayed quipped that the town colors were "tie dye," and yet her establishment was named for the famous Confederate general Thomas "Stonewall" Jackson. The strange juxtaposition of cultures – free-loving 1960's commune-dwelling longhairs and hoary rebel mountain folk – may be best exemplified by the sixteen foot high statue of a Confederate soldier casting his perpetual gaze across the street at a holistic handcrafts boutique and farm-to-table restaurant: the former reminded me of Charlottesville and the latter could've been from any artsy-fartsy West Coast community.

This seeming clash of values was everywhere. The evening we arrived we ate at a fabulous Italian restaurant, and just behind us was a group of three friends. Our tables were so close that not overhearing their conversation was impossible. We hadn't been seated more than five minutes when one of them casually slipped "nigger" into something he said. Peg and I exchanged looks of quiet amazement; neither of us had heard the word in public since we were kids. Then, at the end of their dinner, the same man who said it climbed into a Subaru and drove away, a Human Rights Campaign sticker on his bumper.

This was Floyd in all its motley display of conflicting traditions. Despite the official propaganda from its visitor's bureau implying diversity, we saw nary a black person; to be fair, I did see one individual who looked to be of Asian descent, and there were genuine Spanish-speaking waiters in the Mexican restaurant. But otherwise, Floyd seemed preposterously white. Given the love-culture origins of its most recent inhabitants, that seemed odd.

The area has long been the home to a community of hard-working mountain people, probably best depicted in the 1970 biography of the Rev. Bob Childress, *The Man Who Moved a Mountain*, by Richard Davids. The author describes the culture in great detail, including peculiar nuances of speech. I heard many of them in my mother's everyday talk as a child, although she lost most of them later in life. *Necked*, for naked; *git*, for get; *warsh,* for wash- all seemed strangely mispronounced to me the first time I heard them outside my home. The people of Floyd County were simple, brawling, and proud, but their lives were so harsh that many emigrated for what they hoped to be greener pastures.

Then the Cold War came. Somehow (one person told me it was because of a proclamation by the Dalai Lama, although why His Holiness would know anything about such a remote area of Virginia escapes me), hippies and nuclear-apocalypse survivalists discovered the deep rolling hollows and clear mountain streams of the region and established communes to weather the oncoming bad times. Which never came. But many of the refugees from the outside remained, and they spawned the wonderful arts community of present-day Floyd. The Republic of Floyd Emporium still welcomes visitors with a banner announcing itself as "Your Endtimes Supplier."

The town is amazing, a tiny oasis of bewildering blended cultures. The Crooked Road Music Trail runs right through it, a historical highway-bound celebration of roots and old-timey music; the Floyd events calendar is littered with festivals and live performances. Spontaneous gatherings of acoustic musicians break out on street corners. A neo-hippie ambiance infuses everything, and the spirituality of the inhabitants is unmistakable.

Sally, our hostess, a woman of advanced education who seemed to have done a little bit of everything at one time or another, punctuated her lively conversation with natural references to God's providence. She spoke of praying about life decisions, great or small, in the same unforced tones many of us would use to explain looking on Google. "If God's in it, he's in all of it," I heard her remark numerous times. It didn't matter if she was referring to a life-altering decision or what to make for breakfast. And it was at breakfast that I was again struck by the jarring tension of values...the old and the new, the spiritual and the bigoted.

Another guest, his food initially untouched as Peg and I were beginning ours, said quietly that he and he wife always asked a blessing on the meal. We politely said, "Of course," and put down our forks. They held hands as he spoke a brief direct prayer ending with "Amen," which Peg and I cordially echoed. Then we continued our breakfast. But, again, I couldn't help note the glaring paradox: only minutes earlier the man had been speaking about the "boons" who worked for him. Again, I hadn't heard the word used that way since childhood; it was something my mother occasionally said, an especially derogatory term for black people.

I'd fretted over how to deal with the keepers of the archives I sought, and my experiences in Floyd only deepened my anxiety. Despite the gregarious nature of the people we'd met, it was clear that an undercurrent of not-so-subtle racism was still alive and kicking, if not thriving. I wondered how modern Virginians would respond to my search for evidence of my ancestor and his slave. I was especially nervous about how to approach finding documentation of Price's being freed, but to follow Sally's thinking, God spared me the trial. At least initially.

The morning Peg and I left for Stuart was gorgeous. We'd driven through nonstop rain to reach Floyd only two days before, but now the sky was a dreamy blue, glorified here and there with wispy clouds. The meandering roads from Floyd were uncrowded and smooth, and in forty-five minutes we'd arrived.

Patrick County is right on the state line. In fact, my aunt's history says Alexander II was raised in Stokes County, North Carolina; that's where he met and married Mary Elizabeth Coffee, and it's her headstone we photographed in the Joyce cemetery. Stuart, the seat of Patrick County and the home of the genealogical library, is maybe twice the size of Floyd, and features more nationwide chain stores. It also features something else we hadn't seen in Floyd: people of color.

When we got to the library, a black gentleman was waiting in his car for the building to open. I turned to Peg. "Hopefully that's a good sign," I smiled. I picked up my manila folder of family papers and we went in.

We were greeted by Greg. He was seated at the door behind a big desk covered with papers, files, and books; at least I *think* there was a desk under all of it. Greg was a late middle-aged man in glasses with a shaggy salt-and-pepper beard. He looked like a Civil War reenactor: I easily pictured him in one of the several old uniforms on display around the room, proud sword swinging from his belt. He spoke with the soft, distinct cadences of a librarian, but not with a southern accent. Greg, it turned out, was a slowly displaced northerner, an émigré from first Michigan, then Ohio, presently settled in Virginia.

I laughed. "At this rate, you'll eventually wind up in Miami."

"Probably," he chuckled. "I'm just trying to stay warm."

"Shouldn't be much of a problem, what with climate change and all," I said.

He nodded, and realizing I was dealing with someone who was practically a neighbor, I explained my mission. He quickly moved around the room, pulling enormous binders from the stacks and placing them on a central table. In a matter of minutes Peg and I stood before an impressive collection of material.

"Here you go," he chimed happily. "All having to do with the Joyce family in Patrick County!"

I pressed farther. "I'm particularly interested in anything having to do with a freeman my ancestor brought with him to Indiana."

"Oh," Greg said. He walked off but soon returned, presenting me with a slim book titled *Registration of Free People of Color.*

"This might be helpful," he said.

It wasn't. It was an extensive record of one particular Patrick County family and their slaves, but not *my* family. Greg offered to look through his various computer databases for any mention of Price, and as he typed away furiously, Peg and I sorted through the columns of books in front of us. It didn't prove that difficult; many of them referred to Joyce affairs well after my ancestor left Virginia, and most of the others contained information we already had. It was exhilarating to see the very documents Aunt Flora had looked through when compiling her narrative almost fifty years before, but there was absolutely nothing to support what she'd said about Price being freed, let alone any details of Alexander's exodus. After considerable wheezing on my part and sifting through old documents, the source of her information about the flatboats, the horses, and Price's manumission remained a mystery. The one tantalizing bit of new information Peg found was that the purchaser of Alexander's property was his father-in-law, Richard Coffee. The man had helped to finance his daughter's leaving Virginia, and in all likelihood he never saw her again.

"I can't find anything on Price," Greg said when he returned. "I *may* have found the site of the old mill though, but not on Russell Creek. There's a record of a Joyce Mill on Spencer's Creek, but there's really no way of knowing if it's the right one."

I shut the musty book in front of me, disappointed but not surprised.

I sighed, "I'd hoped to find evidence of Price and his freedom, and I'd hoped to find some explanation for why Alexander left Virginia in the first place." I made a wide gesture. "This area's beautiful."

Greg nodded as someone who'd chosen to live there. "It is, but it's a hard place. It's been said that Patrick County's main export has been its people."

"I wonder why," I mused. Then, "I realize that I'm asking you to speculate, but I respect your speculation: you obviously know this place well. Why would you say my ancestor might've left here? Economic conditions? I mean, given the situation in the country at the time, I'm finding it more difficult to think that he was leaving on humanitarian grounds for Price's sake. Heading for Missouri or Kansas? Or even Indiana? I don't think so."

Greg nodded. "I agree. Indiana's track record with blacks wasn't good, even if it was legally a free state. So, it's pretty unlikely they left for philosophical reasons."

He was quiet for a bit, then asked, "Their land was in the south part of the county?"

"Yeah. Right on the North Carolina line."

"Hmm," he pondered. "Much of that land was used for tobacco crops, and tobacco just destroys the soil. Five or six years and the ground's ruined for anything. And with the economic climate at the time, it could be that he either had to leave or starve."

Now Alexander's selling to his father-in-law made sense. Maybe the elder Coffee was being more charitable than anything else, offering to buy his son-in-law's deflated property in order to provide him and his daughter with a fresh start in the west. If what Greg was saying was accurate, there would've been no scarcity of land to buy in Patrick County.

"I get all that," I said. "That probably explains it. But there's still the unanswered question of Price. What about any court records that might show he was freed?"

"Probably at the courthouse," Greg answered. He pointed out the window and down the street. "Right there," he said, pointing to a big alabaster building. I shook his hand and thanked him. He was happily restacking the books about the Joyce family as Peg and I left for the courthouse.

This was my last shot, I reasoned, emptying my pockets for the trooper attending the body scanner. Peg had sailed right through, but in my nervousness I'd failed to remove my belt, and I set the machine off. I winced as it shrieked.

"Sorry," I apologized weakly as he ran the wand over me.

"You're fine," he answered in a *very* southern accent. I picked my phone and keys out of the basket and rejoined my wife, already on her way into the records room. There, behind a tall reception counter were two women, one white and one black. The white lady asked if she could help.

I was almost overcome with embarrassment.

"Uh…" I stammered. "I'm looking for ancestral records." Then, almost inaudibly, "Especially any records of someone who had been…uh, en*slaved*, then freed." I was mortified as I uttered the word "enslaved."

My wife, however, doesn't suffer from my crippling social ineptitude.

"He's buried in our family cemetery," she sang happily. "And we want to get him a headstone."

"Oh, I see," the white lady said. She turned to the black woman. "I'm going to lunch. You wanna help these folks?"

"She'll take care of you," she said, pulling a shoulder bag from under the counter. "She can help you find anything you need."

I smiled weakly at the woman. "I have no idea what I'm doing."

She smiled back. "Well, let's see what we can find."

In the next room were long storage cases with dozens of enormous registers lying flat. "What year?" she asked. These gigantic binders were handwritten records of the county court's proceedings, arranged in chronological order. The clerks began writing at the front and fill the register, then begin a new one.

"Well," I answered, "we know they were in Indiana by 1830, so we're thinking 1829." She lugged one of the monstrous books from about halfway down the first stack and placed it heavily on top of the cabinet. On the front was inscribed "1850-1854." She put it back and tugged out another one, but shook her head; replacing it, she ran her finger down the spines of the remaining registers in the stack, finally pulling out the very bottom one. It was different from any of the others, far smaller and dog-eared, looking like a guestbook you might sign in a funeral home.

"This is the earliest one," she said with finality.

She placed it in front of me and I touched its tattered cover, brownish-yellow and scaly. Books so old are delicate things, fragile and brittle. I looked at Peg hopefully and slowly opened it. The very first entry on the very first page was dated 1831.

So that was it. My hopes of finding Price and his freedom evaporated in an instant, carried away on the fusty fragrance of the mildewed register's pages. As I shut it gently in frustration, the cover became severed from its spine, seemingly underscoring the disappointment of the moment.

We left Floyd the next morning after yet another of Sally's abundant southern breakfasts. The morning was clear, and a cool, crisp breeze escorted us down the mountains. At the bottom of one crest we saw a double billboard with one final reminder of the conflicting values we'd witnessed the past few days. The top billboard was sponsored by a local church, encouraging the viewer to "Hang out with Jesus, because he hung out for you." Just below it, in glaring neon text, the bottom billboard advertised an adult bookstore.

But despite the cultural dichotomy and my failure to document Price's freedom, I'd fallen in love with Virginia. I'd felt something akin to what I'd felt in Ireland, something like a homecoming. Surrounded by the beauty of the hills and the water, I totally understood that it would be impossible to keep from singing in this place. Leaving the land of my fathers behind me, Peg's car stereo was blasting the soundtrack from *The Greatest Showman*. The cast was singing against an impossibly compelling Celtic rhythm, accompanied by a ringing banjo, and tears were welling up in my eyes-

"And we will come back home, and we will come back home, home again…"

Chapter 4

The Beauty is in the Fruit

On the way home we drove by a big apple orchard.

"The trees look so gnarly," I said, grimacing.

"True," Peg replied. "The beauty's in the fruit."

My wife has a talent for dropping aphorisms that make my mind explode, and her quip churned over and over in my head.

The beauty's in the fruit. The beauty's in the fruit...

I had a lot of time on our drive to process the things I'd recently seen and heard. Her observation about the apple trees struck home; I realized that regardless of the shame and ignominy connected to my family's history of slavery and racism, my task was now clearly before me, not behind. I couldn't change the past. I couldn't even wring a shred of dignity or justification from the historical records to prove that my ancestor has freed his one slave. In fact, given all the circumstantial evidence I'd accumulated, I felt fairly confident that he hadn't. But I was powerless to do anything about that; I could only move forward.

Because the beauty is in the fruit. The roots and branches may be a twisted, contorted, ugly mess, but they can produce something of goodness, something of wonder: they can produce redemption.

Heather Heyer's mother had encouraged us all to look the evil of racism right in the face, and then do something: she had called on us to make a difference. Regardless of whether I was able to document Price's freedom and willingness to accompany Alexander to Indiana, and regardless of whether I could even prove that he rested unrecognized under the soil of our tiny family cemetery, I still could do *something*. And if what I did was to stand any chance of making any difference, it would have to be a public act, something not done simply for my own edification.

Because the beauty's in the fruit.

I was ready to present my case to the Franklin Township trustee, the person with the authority to approve placing a headstone for Price in the graveyard. Here's what I planned to say, and after all my research, what I currently believed-

Sometime in 1829, my ancestor, Alexander Joyce II, sold his property in Patrick County, Virginia, to his father-in-law, Richard Coffee of Stokes County, North Carolina. The parcel consisted of two hundred acres with a mill, which may have been on Russell Creek. It was probably a multi-purposed facility, processing both local timber and grain, driven by the powerful rushing creek waters.

Alexander had been left the property with the mill by his father, also an Alexander, along with a sorrel mare and a slave boy named Price. These are all specifically noted in the elder Alexander's will of 1817. We have no idea how old Price may have been or what his specific relationship to Alexander II was. We know Alexander II was fully fecund: he and Mary Elizabeth Coffee had nine children together.

We can't be certain why Alexander chose to leave Virginia. We do know that the entire country was in the grips of its first major economic crisis, that banks and businesses were failing, loans were being suddenly called in, and credit was being radically curbed. It's also likely that Alexander may have been a tobacco farmer, and it's entirely possible that his land, after years of raising a crop that emaciates the soil, had become useless for growing anything at all. It's likely that any contract business he'd conducted at his mill was curtailed because of the hard times; combined with the likely failure of his crops, the lure of the west may have become irresistible.

And there may have been other contributing factors to his deciding to move…family tensions, wanderlust. We simply don't know and probably never will. We do know that Alexander's decision wasn't unique. During that period and for decades after, the hill people of Patrick County left their homes in droves for other climes.

My great-aunt provides details of Alexander's exodus that I have been unable to confirm, among them the notions that all but one his children accompanied him, that he built two flatboats carrying wagons and household possessions, that there were eight horses (probably for pulling the boats) and – most notably – that the slave boy, Price, was freed and subsequently asked permission to remain with the family on their journey. If Price were legally freed in Virginia by means of the issuance of a Certificate of Manumission, I've been unable to locate any record of it. I've concluded on circumstantial evidence that such a court proceeding probably never took place.

After all, what would've been Alexander's motivation to legally free Price? At the very least it would have been a nuisance to do so- filling out paperwork, appearing before the court, probably paying some sort of court costs, all to take a single slave to a state where he would've been free regardless of his status in Virginia. Indiana's 1816 constitution explicitly says so: no "indenture" of any "negro or mulatto" "executed out of the bounds of this state" will "be of any validity." Price became free, if still hobbled by strident legal sanctions, once he crossed the Indiana state line. My great aunt, in relaying the family lore, may have innocently expanded this legal technicality into the story that Alexander "freed" Price.

And frankly, while it causes me considerable shame to say so, when I consider the historical and cultural nuances of the time, I think the most likely scenario is that Alexander had no intention of freeing him at all. Aunt Flora's narrative suggests that Alexander and his family were heading for Kansas, which most decidedly wasn't a free territory like Ohio or (ostensibly) Indiana; there's also a flawed redaction of the story told by my grandmother and transcribed by my aunt that says their destination was St. Louis, one of main centers of the slave trade in the entire country.

Most likely, if Price wasn't sold to Alexander's father-in-law along with the land and the mill, he went with the family when they left Virginia because he was *still* their slave, relocating to a slave state, simply because life in Patrick County had become unsustainable. Meaning to go further west, the family was stopped on their journey by the freezing of the Ohio River and they set themselves up in southern Indiana to pass the winter. For some reason, unknown to us, they didn't go further for a couple of years: they appear in the Jefferson County census of 1830...all but Price.

I would contend that the reason Price isn't mentioned is because he remained a slave, even in the constitutionally free land of Indiana. It's historically inarguable that a great deal of slavery still existed *de facto* in the state, and to have included the black man's name in the census would've been to openly declare his presence and freedom. When Alexander purchased his parcel of land farther north in 1832, forty acres in Johnson County and forty acres in Marion County, Price probably went with the family as well, still a slave: he remains absent from the census rolls in 1840, an invisible sojourner in a land where he was forbidden to call anything his own.

This is all conjecture on my part, extrapolated from incomplete and conflicting family stories and history. The available documentation makes concluding anything definite very difficult. It's *possible* that what I once believed is true, that Alexander wanted to free Price out of the goodness of his heart, and that his moving from Virginia was because he wanted to resettle in an area free from slavery. There were a few Quakers in southern Virginia in the early 19th century, and they may have influenced his thinking. But it's not likely. A betting person would wager in favor of my analysis, that a son-of-a-son-of-a-son-of-a-son of a southern slaver was an inveterate slaver too.

The earliest gravestone in the Joyce cemetery records a death in 1846, Jesse King, related to Alexander by marriage. Alexander II died in 1862 and sleeps next to his wife, Mary, who died eight years earlier. The most recent marker is from 1980. There are fifteen noted graves in all.

But in the most remote corner of that tiny graveyard, deposited as far away as possible from the lovingly marked bodies of the white people he served his entire life, I believe is the final resting place of a black man named Price. Price Joyce.

And I became obsessed that he would not be forgotten.

I had never purchased a headstone before. Efficient and organized to the end, my mother had bought her own when my father passed, sparing my brothers and I the task. It felt odd walking into the office of Greenfield Granite, shopping for a marker for someone who had died generations ago, someone I really knew almost nothing about.

Peg and I entered through a back door. The place had an old-timey craftsman's-shop feel about it; there were stones in various stages of preparation, wooden sawhorses, and cast-aside tools. A man was performing some indeterminate task on a stone; he looked up.

"Can we help you?" he inquired routinely.

"Uh," I stammered, always uncomfortable discussing my project with strangers, "We need to speak to someone about a gravestone."

"Sure," he said, dropping a tool on the monolith in front of him. "This way." We followed him through a hoary abused door into the front reception area. There, a handful of people were sitting around a Formica-topped table eating lunch. One of them. Amie, wiped at her mouth with a paper napkin and stood up to greet us. After introductions she asked, "And who is the deceased?"

"Well," I replied, gathering my wits, "this may be a unique situation."

I really don't know if Amie and the others thought it was unique at all; if they did, they didn't show it. They all listened politely and examined my sketch of what I had in mind with professional detachment. Amie showed us various stones; I initially had thought a simple low-profile marker would be the most appropriate, although I soon changed my mind. We discussed costs, which would include their setting the stone on a concrete base in the cemetery. After thirty minutes or so we left. I felt that I had everything I could possibly muster to meet with the township trustee.

But I kept second-guessing myself. I wanted to be as organized and persuasive as possible with the trustee, who I assumed would be a perfunctory bureaucrat, skeptical at best, scathing at worse. I grew increasingly nervous about the encounter, so I decided that I wanted one more video of my witching the gravesite, no more than few seconds long, something that would be directly to the point. One cool sunny Sunday late in April, we tossed our rat terrier, Doris, in the back seat of Peg's car and set out for the cemetery.

As we pulled into the tank storage lot I was disappointed to see a good-sized utility truck with a long cherry picker parked next to the cemetery gate; a worker was in the basket trimming tree limbs with a chain saw. A second worker was gathering the debris, and a third stood next to the truck, watching it all. I realized I probably wasn't going to be able to shoot my witching video, but since we'd already been spotted by the three, we decided to walk up anyway.

"Getting things shaped up?" I said to the guy beside the truck, trying to sound cheerier than I was. He looked to be about my age, with grizzled chin whiskers and dark sunglasses. "These are all my ancestors," I offered in explanation, gesturing at the headstones.

"That right?" he answered, unimpressed.

"Yeah," still trying to establish my authenticity, "My mother was a Joyce."

"Huh," he grunted, looking up at the man with the chain saw. "Be sure to get those two over there," be barked, pointing at a couple of wayward limbs.

"We just set the flagpole today," he said, not looking at me. For the first time I noticed the tall white mast planted in the center of the cemetery. It seemed jarring to me...out of place in this ancient family burial ground.

"Oh," I said, hoping I hadn't betrayed my disappointment. An awkward silence followed. "There's a slave buried in here," I said after a bit.

He turned back to me, interested for the first time. "You know, I've heard that."

This seemed encouraging. "Yeah, we just got back from Virginia, trying to locate any court records. Got mixed results."

More silence. Doris sniffed at the guy's boots.

"Rat terrier," I said.

"Uh-huh," he mumbled, looking elsewhere. I pressed on.

"I'm trying to put a case together to present to the Franklin Township trustee. I'd like to put a headstone in here...for the slave. We know his name, but that's about it. The trustee maintains the grounds now. Does a good job, too. It was a mess for years."

"Oh, I know," he said.

"Really? You work for the trustee?"

"I *am* the trustee," he smiled.

And this, I realized, might turn out to be a fortuitous turn of events.

Clifford Kight, known to everyone as "Cookie," hadn't been elected trustee, but a friend of his had. When the friend died in office, Cookie agreed to serve out his term. Cookie is a man who gets things done, and I strongly suspect he has a very low tolerance for fools.

Before we left the cemetery – I didn't attempt to shoot a video, given the circumstances – I asked if I could talk with him more another time. He suggested I stop by his auto body repair shop in Acton. We shook hands: I said in parting that I was very glad to meet him. And I was.

Two days later I drove back into the tiny town and found his place, a long low building festooned with crazy-carnival block letters declaring "COOKIE'S." I made my way from the front entrance to a tiny office; the air hung thick in a forest of car parts and abandoned tools, heavy with the smell of paint solvents and grease.

The little office was a throwback to the mid-60's…wood paneling crowned by a suspended ceiling and glaring fluorescent lights, Naugahyde-and-chrome chairs, and an ancient laminated counter obscured with countless purchase orders and invoices. A mute boar's head hung high on the wall watching the Fox news channel; American flags in various sizes were displayed everywhere.

A young woman behind the counter was talking on the phone. It was around 2 in the afternoon and there was a problem getting delivery on some doodad needed for a repair.

"Well, I promised it to him today," she said, not angrily but firmly, "so what time…" She listened to the squawking on the other end, then quipped, "All right, then. Thanks."

She jotted down a quick note on a slip in the pandemonium of papers, then looked at me, smiling, "Yes?"

"Cookie here?" I asked, smiling back.

"No, he's already gone," she answered, nudging the flotsam around as though it might spontaneously organize itself. "He usually leaves around noon. He's got COPD and the fumes..." she waved her hand toward the shop, her gesture completing her thought.

"Maybe I can help you? I'm Heather, his daughter."

"Oh, good," I said. "I ran into him at that little Joyce cemetery Sunday and I was hoping to talk him a little about it. It's looking really good these days. They were setting up a flagpole."

Heather smiled. "We're *very* patriotic," she said in a proud tone. "We've been putting flag poles in all the old cemeteries."

"All?" I asked. She had me a trifold pamphlet.

"I just got these back this morning." The front cover read

Pioneer Cemeteries
of Franklin Township

Maintained by the Franklin Township
Trustees Office

I unfolded it and saw seven tiny cemeteries listed; the last one was ours.

"That's wonderful," I said, slipping the pamphlet into my notebook. "Any idea when he might be in?"

"He usually comes in around 9 o'clock. His number's on the back of the pamphlet. Give him a call. I'm sure he'd be happy to talk to you."

I called, and a week later, right at 9, I was back in the little office. The boar's head and I watched Fox together, awaiting Cookie's arrival. We didn't wait long.

I've dealt with bureaucrats before. I've had to appear before commissions and tedious panels more than once when seeking permission to build in a historical district in Indianapolis. In preparing my case I had assembled multiple copies of my research, my summation, and designs for the headstone. I'd even queued up the video of my witching the suspected burial spot on my phone. And it all proved unnecessary

Cookie, in his demeanor, was casual and *anything* but formal. As we sat across from each other in his office with the morning's headlines scrolling over and over and Heather and the boar's head eavesdropping nearby, the trustee reminded me of nothing so much as my late father-in-law. I saw a working man of the oldest school, part craftsman and part entrepreneur, grizzled and scarred by decades at the grindstone. I rubbed my own calloused fingers together and imagined Cookie's hands to be as leathery as my own.

I realized it was possible, maybe even likely, that he'd known my wife's father; after all, both Peg's family and the Kights – and for that matter, my own – had been fixtures in southern Marion and northern Johnson counties for generations. I chose not to play the familial card though, since one never quite knew how it might fall. I left my neatly prepped and collated papers in the folder beside me and softly slid into an adlibbed - and *brief* – presentation of my connection to the cemetery and Price. Cookie listened quietly.

"I've heard about the slave," he repeated. "I was talking to the woman who owns the property the cemetery's on and she said she'd always heard that too." When he mentioned the woman's name, I recognized it from some of my earliest research; I briefly panicked, thinking Cookie might not have the authority I thought he did.

"So, it's her responsibility? She takes care of it?"

"No, no," Cookie shook his head, picking at a fingernail. "The township handles all of that, but as a courtesy I keep her in the loop."

"I see," I said, relieved. "You know, I tried to find the slave's headstone, but I never could, and now I think he probably never had one."

"Nope," Cookie agreed. "They almost never did. Maybe a wooden cross or a tree planted close, but otherwise…"

"I'd like to put one in there for him," I blurted out. Cookie looked up at me. "I think I know where he is," I said.

"How?" he squinted. I told him.

I've consistently found over the years that almost no one I tell about my ability to witch seems surprised or doubts me, and Cookie was no different.

"Right in that back corner, huh?"

"Yep. My daughter can do the rods too, and she got hits back there as well. In fact, we both got indications on three sites around that wooden bench."

I let it sink in.

"I think that'd be fine," he finally said. "Got a design?" I pulled out the diagram I'd done and passed it to him.

As he looked it over I tried to judge his expression, but found it inscrutable.

The next few seconds dragged. This was it; this was the moment I'd been dogging toward for the biggest part of a year. I looked around the office, at Heather, at the ancient paneling, at the relentless Fox news anchor, at the boar's head and American flags.

"I think that'd be real nice," he said, handing the sketch back to me.

"You can keep that," I said, feeling water coming to my eyes. "It's for you." I explained that I'd cover all the expenses and told him about Greenfield Granite. His only request was that the stone be upright, not flat, in order to more closely match the style of the other stones. I agreed instantly; I would've agreed to almost anything. I was ecstatic.

We talked a bit more before I left. I learned that he was a committed supporter of the 2nd Amendment, and in reaction to something on the TV, he advised me to stay "locked and loaded," assuring me that "the revolution is coming." In parting he told me with grim conspiratorial irony "We're the survivors. We got ass whippin's and drank water from the hose." I assured him I'd keep him updated and that I'd get his approval for the final design of the stone.

"I'm sure it'll be fine," he said as we shook hands. I drove away, thrilled with the outcome of the brief meeting and I realized Cookie had been absolutely right: I *had* survived ass whippin's and hose water. Truth be told, I *still* occasionally drink from the hose.

Late in June, after several exchanges about design with Amie, I got the go-ahead from Cookie. The summer scorched past and autumn crept in. I knew the process of getting a gravestone carved would be lengthy, but I was surprised at how long it ultimately took.

On the 5th of November I was rebuilding a rotted-out deck behind a condominium on the north side of Indianapolis. It was a good-sized project, about as big as anything I tackle these days, so I was grateful for the interruption when the phone rang a little after noon. It was Amie.

"We got the stone put in this morning. My husband says it looks very nice." I told her I was sure it did and repeatedly thanked her. I packed up my tools, jumped in my truck, and headed for Acton. As I wound around the narrow drive and parked among the giant gas tanks, I was close to trembling. My walk through the recently cut pasture seemed especially long; it was the end of a journey I'd first started at my mother's knee.

I wondered what she would think as I pushed open the gate. I wondered what she would think of the lengths to which I'd gone to honor this phantom, this black man. Would she think it was foolish? Would she be proud? Would she complain that I never visit *her* grave? And then there it was…cool and polished, glistening silver granite proudly upright in the precise spot I'd indicated. There had been heavy rain earlier in the week, and I sat cross-legged in the mud before the stone and sobbed. I don't know why. I've never known why this affair has affected me the way it has.

I stood after several minutes and gently touched Price's stone, then I walked out, pulling the gate creakily behind me. As I stepped into my truck at 3 in the afternoon, I whispered to no one in particular, "Thank you."

Chapter 5
Taking the 12th Step

I'm not a sociologist or historian. I hold no academic credentials that entitle me to analyze our country's ancient curse of racism. I possess no accreditation that might persuade anyone that I know how to remedy it. I'm a carpenter, a carpenter with a family history that includes slaveholding and a mysterious diaspora, and I'm willing to publicly acknowledge it. If I possess any unique ability to speak to the issue at all, it's only because I've spent a great deal of time reflecting on it. It may be closer to the truth to say I've obsessed over it, because of my ancestry, and here's what I've concluded.

While the contours of racism may have been redrawn in the past half century, it's still woven deeply into our national fabric. I suspect if, by some magic wave of a wand, the racist strands could be made to disappear, we'd be shocked at what a tattered and bedraggled cloth would remain. Perhaps the most astonishing aspect of America's racism is that while portions of our citizenry are profoundly and painfully conscious of it, there are concurrently enormous segments who don't appear to be conscious of it at all. Our national pigmentation is becoming darker all the time, and many white people, especially those of my generation, sometimes feel disoriented and confused by it.

We hear the term "white privilege" a lot and, depending on your perspective, you may bristle and take offense, claiming that it's a convenient political chimera, or sadly nod your head in grim affirmation of its reality. For people of color, it's an undeniable reality of life; for white folk, it's practically imperceptible, and I think I know why.

My wife's left-handed. With some notable exceptions, she's been forced into a life of mercilessly enforced ambidexterity and she's survived, even thrived, despite it. She writes left-handed and pitches softball left-handed, but curiously she bats right-handed, as she does most everything else. For decades I've watched her struggle to navigate as a southpaw in a brutally right-handed world.

There used to be a little left-handed boutique in our downtown mall, and she was thrilled to discover it. Its shelves held left-handed rulers and notebooks and cooking utensils, even scissors. Who knew?

"Look!" she squealed on one occasion, "A left-handed coffee cup!"

"What?" I said, incredulous. "How can a cup be right- or left-handed?"

"See?" she said, brandishing it at me in her left hand. It featured some pun about only left-handed people being in their right mind. I took it in my right hand and immediately noticed that the cute pun was now invisible: the surface I could see was blank; the joke was now displayed away from me, like the dark side of the moon.

"Huh," I remarked. "I had no idea."

Take a minute to look around you, righties. School desks are right-handed, cash registers and checkout lines are right-handed, letter openers, pencil sharpeners, butter knives- all right-handed. We use them every day and think nothing of it; we notice nothing remarkable in their orientation. But if you ever sit at a left-handed school desk – and there are a few out there - it's a jarring experience. It looks wrong, slightly demented, like something from a Lewis Carroll looking-glass world.

For years I've thought it would be cool to create an entirely left-handed environment, maybe for a children's museum or something, so right-handed people could experience what lefties must put up with every day. Even though left-handed people make up about 10 percent of the population, the world we've built shamelessly favors the right-handed, and there's plenty of good research that indicates lefties have unique health issues and even die – on average – earlier than righties.

My point is this: while individuals like my functionally-ambidextrous wife fully appreciate what I'm saying, in all likelihood it's something that most right-handed people have never even considered. They don't have to.

Just like white privilege.

It's easy to pooh-pooh the notion of a systemic cultural bias against a minority when you're part of the majority. You simply never see it. I never think about its inherent utility and convenience when I pick up a knife to slather butter on my dinner roll. I also never think that I'm being watched with greater scrutiny when I step into a department store or worry that I'm more likely to be stopped by a cop when I'm driving my car. Because I'm not. But a black man is.

I once listened in fascinated horror to a white suburban police officer say with great alacrity that he never passed up the opportunity to pull over any black man driving though his district. (He didn't say "black man," by the way, but used another term that left no doubt what he meant.) Maybe even more disturbing was the fact that he was making his observations to a second white officer who just nodded his head in assent. If there ever was more scurrilous corroboration of the concept of being stopped for DWB (driving while black), I've never heard it.

As white people we don't want to believe we're the unwitting beneficiaries of a rigged system. We want to believe that the rewards we reap from our participation in American society are fairly won, that our hard work and honest efforts are what ultimately lead to our success. But the honest truth is that about 12 percent of our population is pursuing happiness hobbled. White privilege is pervasive and systemic and particularly insidious, because almost nine-tenths of the population rarely sees it, and many will claim that it doesn't even exist.

And it's not just that white privilege deniers are blind to the truth, but their blindness manifests in assertions of "reverse discrimination," mass black incarceration, gerrymandering and restriction of voters' rights, curtailing of affirmative action quotas, and – most tragically – police action shootings in which unarmed black men are the targets.

I'm not going to recite the litany of names that comprise this category of violence that has become a mainstay of our news cycles. I'm not an advocate for any special interest group or political organization, but you'd have to be living in a sealed crypt not to notice that a disproportionate number of these shootings seem questionable. The only thing the victim consistently appears to be guilty of is Failure to be White. And I suspect it's all fundamentally fueled by fear, the same fear others tried to instill in me as a little kid in Florida when they assured me that any black person I saw on the street would be happy to hack me to death with their surreptitious shivs.

So, this is where I'm going to venture into dangerous and controversial territory, since I have little documentable evidence for the assertions I'm about to make, other than my own observations and introspection. I'd just ask you to at least entertain my suggestions, and perhaps you'll find something among them to incorporate into your own process as you triangulate our troubled racial waters.

I strongly suspect that many white people *still* live in fear of black folk, and I think it's something more than the xenophobia that exists among all people.*   I suspect, but cannot prove, that America's particular brand of racism is a sickness that has deep, deep roots in our country's unique history, a history involving the enslavement and exploitation of Africans by whites, a tragic civil war of catastrophic proportions, followed by a long period of systematic repression of the allegedly freed slaves.

Price, as an example, was "free" when he crossed into Indiana with Alexander, but it was a sham freedom constructed of legalistic jargon, an only-on-paper kind of freedom. It was freedom in principle, but hardly in practice. Any black individual coming into our state had to have a white "sponsor," someone who would

---

*I highly recommend Steven Pinker's extremely well-researched and wonderfully readable book, *The Better Angels of Our Nature*. He cites a large body of evidence that suggests that while we truly aren't born prejudiced, we begin to develop strong racial preference by 6 months of age. Tribalism is an essential part of our species' makeup and will probably always be; but *bigotry* – the wholesale demonization of an entire group of people – is most certainly not.

vouch for and promise to financially secure the other's endeavors. In essence, the black man had to have a master, even if it wasn't called that.

And after the north's victory in the Civil War, people of color were kept terrified in their place by groups like the Klan and the broad practice of accountability-free lynching, even in Indiana, which – constitutionally – had always been a free state. It's a badge of particular infamy that the incident that led to the composition of Billie Holiday's signature song, *Strange Fruit*, took place in Marion, Indiana in 1930 when two black men were tortured with hammers and then hanged from a tree on the courthouse square.

On the *courthouse square*. Let that sink in a moment.

I believe the KKK and lynching, as well as our current practice of mass incarceration of black men and police action shootings, are all born out of fear, a historically-grounded fear that comes from deep within white people…a fear that people of African descent may very well have a *right* to retribution. White people exist in a great fog of fear, and I wonder if the *de facto* repression that persists in our culture isn't because whites understand that, in one form or another, we've got it coming. Is it possible that our racial fear grows from our underlying sense of guilt, the blood-guilt that we've carried for generations?

It really doesn't matter if white folks embrace the notions of white privilege and blood-guilt, because

black folks do, and all our denials and protestation can't change that.

Undoubtedly it would be helpful if we could adjust perceptions on both sides of the racial divide. Undeniably, not all whites are looking to hobble and string blacks up, figuratively or otherwise, nor are all African Americans gun-toting, blade-wielding thugs who want to indiscriminately murder whites. To be sure, either of those ugly stereotypes represents only tiny fringe elements within their respective race, but the stereotypes continue to play across the collective consciousness. But *why*, particularly at a time when we're more aware of racial inequities than we've ever been? The answer is partly in a fundamental dichotomy within the human spirit.

I've never met anyone outside a casket who wasn't a complete and persistent hypocrite. The very essence of the human condition is to live as a perpetual paradox. Plato claimed that if we could rationally determine the right moral course, we would inevitably take it. On the other hand, St. Paul questioned why he seemed to be unable to behave morally even when he knew precisely how to. We *know* that our racist inclinations are destructive and need to be purged from our social transactions, but we cling to them anyway. Why?

I'm not sure it matters. While discovering why we display destructive behaviors may help to fill in blank spaces in our biographies, it isn't essential to correcting the behaviors.

A few years ago I picked up a guy who had spent the night in a county lockup after being arrested in the wee hours of the morning for drunk driving. It turned out to be his first and only arrest, and as I drove him home he pilloried himself for doing such a foolish thing. There had been several previous incidents when he'd had too much drink and had behaved foolishly, but this time he'd wound up in jail.

"I just don't understand why I do such things," he said, shaking his head in frustration.

"You really don't?" I asked.

"No," he moaned. He was genuinely mystified.

"Because," I said with earnest finality, "you're an alcoholic."

He was silent for a good time, letting the full force of what I'd said sink in. We talked a great deal more after that, and to this day he's not taken another drink. He joined AA, found a no-nonsense sponsor, worked the program, and now has many years of sobriety behind him.

His arrest ended up costing him thousands of dollars, great embarrassment, and profound inconvenience. But he didn't invest a lot of energy in trying to figure out *why* he was an alcoholic; instead, he began with that basic admission and then worked to change his behavior. In my experience, individuals who spend a great deal of time trying to figure out the why of the situation are often looking for loopholes…get-out-of-jail-free passes. Many addicts have relapsed because they thought they could harness the beast and tame it. But I don't know that you can. I think you must kill it outright.

Changing the behavior is paramount. If your house is on fire, the proper time to determine how it started is *after* you put out the flames.

I've made no secret of my fondness for the 12-Step paradigm propagated by Alcoholics Anonymous. Dr. Bob, Bill W., and their friends discovered decades ago that a mindful, confessional, and accountable approach to the demon of alcohol was – if consistently practiced – an effective remedy to its deadly grip. I've found the 12 Steps helpful, as I've told many a troubled parent, realizing that his or her child was far deeper down the path of addiction than they might have realized. And I've found them to be helpful in the process of confronting my racism. But for all of us, you have to work the program for the program to work.

The 12 Steps weren't handed down on tablets, complete and dogmatically sealed. AA's founders spent a great deal of time refining the final list; sometimes there were more than twelve, sometimes there were fewer. The classic set first published in 1939 has been rewritten, updated, and paraphrased many times. Now it's applicable to destructive behaviors other than alcoholism; in general, the 12 Steps can be brought to bear on any behavior that can be viewed as addictive

But I'd like to make an even more sweeping claim: I believe the 12 Step approach can probably be useful in taking on *any* destructive behavior, at least when the paradigm is reduced to its most basic components. I've called myself a recovering racist. I still harbor racist inclinations that emerge under certain circumstances, but I fully understand that these inclinations are a negative element in my life and damaging to the fabric of the society in which I live. And that understanding is the beginning of recovery.

Here are the 12 Steps in their classic form-

1. We admitted we were powerless over alcohol—that our lives had become unmanageable.
2. Came to believe that a Power greater than ourselves could restore us to sanity.
3. Made a decision to turn our will and our lives over to the care of God as we understood Him.

4. Made a searching and fearless moral inventory of ourselves.

5. Admitted to God, to ourselves, and to another human being the exact nature of our wrongs.

6. Were entirely ready to have God remove all these defects of character.

7. Humbly asked Him to remove our shortcomings.

8. Made a list of all persons we had harmed, and became willing to make amends to them all.

9. Made direct amends to such people wherever possible, except when to do so would injure them or others.

10. Continued to take personal inventory and when we were wrong promptly admitted it.

11. Sought through prayer and meditation to improve our conscious contact with God as we understood Him, praying only for knowledge of His will for us and the power to carry that out.

12. Having had a spiritual awakening as the result of these steps, we tried to carry this message to alcoholics, and to practice these principles in all our affairs. *(© Alcoholics Anonymous)*

Many moderns find the language staid and quaint, and more than a few are put off by the overtly theistic element. It's always seemed to me that the 12 Steps, while perhaps not entirely arbitrary, can be boiled down to more essential components, and that's where their utility as a tool against racism has been helpful to me.

Mindfulness

We're commonly warned in everyday discourse against "self-diagnosis." It's generally a mistake in medical matters to rely on one's own assessment. Only a physician – maybe more than one – can make a genuine evaluation of our condition.

But one possible exception is addiction, at least from the 12 Step recovery perspective. Just as religions split into sects and factions shortly after their founding, 12 Steppers are no different. Many in the recovery culture will disagree with what I'm about to say, but I would assert that for the 12 Steps to work at all, only the addict himself can make the diagnosis. It's imperative that the alcoholic claim his alcoholism for himself. Just like the fabled lonesome valley, the addict has to walk it himself. Nobody else can walk it for him.

Often, local gatherings require two things to gain entrance to an AA meeting: you can't be drunk, and you have to be an alcoholic. The first parameter is typically self-evident, and no one will ever check your documentation for the second. Your word is good enough. *Your* word…not your doctor's, not your spouse's, not your employer's. The alcoholic diagnoses himself; no one else can.

That's the entire thrust of the first step: the individual himself must come to the realization that he needs help, that alcohol is stronger than he is, and that his life has become a shambles. The individual must be able to have the mindfulness to recognize his own desperate need.*

Mindfulness is a quality well known to systems like Buddhism, where deliverance comes by means of becoming aware of one's own inner environment, even to the point of mastering processes that initially appear well beyond the scope of rational control. By ruthlessly scrutinizing the content of one's own perceptions and apperceptions, the mindful can drop their breathing to almost nothing, withstand hours of exposure to sub-zero temperatures, or even self-immolate.

Fortunately, the form of mindfulness I'm recommending for my present purposes is nothing quite so heroic: in order for the addict to begin recovery, he merely needs to fully accept his dependence on his drug of choice.

And the racist needs to genuinely accept that his racism is real and damaging. The alcoholic must truly desire change, and so must the racist. Sadly, we live in a culture that values the wholesale consumption of alcohol; we also live in a culture where, through the systemic propagation of white privilege and denial of its racist substrate, it's probably easier to accept one's alcoholism than one's racism.

*Most everyone is familiar with the notion of "hitting bottom," or finally coming to a pass in your life when your addiction is either going to get you locked away, kill you, or kill someone else. Those with the ability and grace to do it, realize the only route back to sanity is sobriety.

The present effort is probably little more than preaching to the choir, but the choir doesn't show up just to sing. It also shows up to be energized and invigorated, encouraged and heartened. I harbor no illusions that my story will pry some hardened race-hater out of his hole into a more accepting light of day, but maybe it will help others to understand the climate in which we currently find ourselves. I'll come back to this shortly. For now, the point is to emphasize that unless the racist comes to see – by whatever means – that his racism is counter-productive in his life and in his world, he'll never surrender it. Our racist attitudes go to the very core of who we see ourselves to be, particularly in relief against the rest of the world: it literally may be a matter of coming to understand that everything we ever thought is wrong.

Many alcoholics believe that alcohol is essential for them to negotiate life. One guy told me that he needed to drink "just to feel normal." The thought of facing the world sober is terrifying. Giving up one's racist notions can be frightening as well, but in a more existential sense. The mindfulness that leads to the epiphany that one's bigotry is nothing more than an elaborate centuries-old deception may not only be clarifying, it may be jarring as well. Once the reliable footholds of prejudice are gone, the world suddenly seem a slippery and uncertain place. But it also becomes a place of unlimited possibility.

Confession

For more than twenty years I helped to form new Catholics as an adult catechist, and it often fell to me to discuss the sacrament of reconciliation, colloquially called "confession," and that was usually a difficult sell. We never like to admit to our shortcomings, faults, or - for lack of a better term – sins, but the act of doing so *to another human being* can often be one of the most therapeutic acts we can ever perform. The act of confession, particularly as it's embodied in the sacrament, is a path to closure and healing.

Sometimes to the horror of my catechetical colleagues, I would sit in front of our class across from a priest and do a confession…for real, not pretend. The results were usually profound; sometimes I ended up in tears and often members of the group would as well. Always, after I received absolution, the room would be heavily silent. I would eventually break the silence to explain what had just happened, always emphasizing the rejuvenating aspect of it. Confession is good for the soul. It's as simple as that, but we're generally loathe to avail ourselves of it.

Steps 4 through 10 of AA's 12 Steps relate in one way or another to confession…taking a "fearless and searching" inventory of one's acts; admitting our harmful deeds to another; making amends to all individuals we can think of, sometimes in the form of an apology, sometimes in the form of restitution, sometimes both; and continuing to keep our fingers tightly on our moral pulse, being ready to admit our wrongs as soon as we become aware of them.

This is tough stuff. Often, in the process of navigating these steps, people drop out of the program. Confronting one's shortcomings or "defects of character" can prove too intimidating. And the prospect of making amends, face-to-face, to a specific individual can simply seem impossible. * This process is not for the faint of heart, and the irony is, you can't even fortify yourself with a drink first.

But here's the thing: *A History of Racism* is my public confession to anyone who wishes to hear it. I am horribly ashamed of my earliest racist sentiments, and I am mortified by the racist practices of my ancestors. I wish I could make them all evaporate, discharge them into the dustbins of history, but I can't. I genuinely believe that slavery and the practices of white terrorism that followed it remain the gravest sins of our nation, and we're reaping the hideous harvest of those sins to this very day. But, for me and my house, it stops *here*. It stops *now*. I confess to the blood-guilt: I own it, and it's a burden I have carried for a very long time. I am sorry…deeply sorry.

*Once, an employee of mine who was going through the program, made an amends to me from the other side of a closed door, similar to the way penitents used to be on one side of a screen that separated them from their confessors. I couldn't even really understand what he was saying, but I knew what he was doing, and I supported his efforts. He never drank again until the day he died.

Accountability

Which brings me to the final component of the 12 Steps, seeking accountability.

I believe I *have* had a "spiritual awakening" regarding my racism. There's no denying that it's there: it's part of who I am, just like my alcoholism, but it no longer needs to be the filter through which I view the world and my fellow humans. It can be an element of my past that can be labeled, catalogued, and filed away into a locker filled with similar useless and destructive elements. It no longer dictates my perceptions.

And that's good, but it's not enough. For me, seeking atonement is essential. Referring back to Susan Bro, I have seen something and now I must say something; I can't look the other way or ignore the conclusions I've reached. I need to make them public, and this book, along with the headstone in the Joyce Cemetery, is my forum. The 12th Step speaks of carrying the message of sobriety to other alcoholics. In other circles, it might be called evangelization, the spreading of the good news. This book is my attempt to do just that.

If, as I've concluded, Alexander never freed Price, but instead brought him in bondage to just another place of *de facto* enslavement to die and be buried unacclaimed, then maybe *I* can complete the act of liberation that family lore led me to believe took place back in

Virginia. Maybe *I* can free him; but, more to the point, maybe he can free *me*.

Epilogue
Freedom

I want to believe the old stories. I want to believe that Alexander was a magnanimous, progressive, charitable man. I want to believe what I had been told as a boy, that Alexander freed Price before leaving Patrick County and Price, because of his love for Alexander and the Joyce family, chose to remain with them as they sought a new life. But I don't. Particularly when viewed among the other mistaken assertions in our family's recounting, it just doesn't add up. What I believe is that Price was born and died a slave, the "property" of my ancestor, hidden in the farthest corner of the family plot, cut off and abandoned, just as he had been in life. And this belief tears at my soul.

I've said I don't understand why this story moves me, why the tale of this faceless black man, generations dead, can move me to tears. The fact that Price has haunted me so has always confused me, but I think I may be beginning to understand.

It's not just that my sense of empathy is growing deeper as I grow older, although that's part of it. As we age and our hide becomes blemished with greater and deeper scars, we sometimes begin to achieve a certain wisdom: the failure to die is occasionally rewarded by insight that the young are incapable of. But it's not that. Price has always called to me, from the very first time my mother told me of him. His ghost has been my constant traveling companion, sometimes more apparent, sometimes less. The dead – particularly the wrongfully dead – are a persistent bunch. They will not be denied.

In the past few years, as I've watched my country slide into greater factionalism and division, as I've listened to our leaders spit bile and bigotry from their bully pulpits, as I've witnessed Nazis marching and murdering on our streets, Price's presence has loomed larger for me. He has visited me at night, during the day, at work and at leisure; he's visited me on foreign shores and in the clutch of my dearest surroundings. He doesn't accuse; he doesn't reproach. He just gazes at me, eyes full of sadness and a longing I can't fathom.

Does he long for his mother? A lover? I've always imagined him to be about fourteen when he was forced from Virginia, but I've found no documentation to corroborate that assumption. Does he pine for homelands he never knew, grassy green savannahs far across an unimaginable ocean, conjured up to him around firelight by keepers of memories? I don't know.

A pastor friend of mine has suggested that I love him, that I love this ancient colored man I know only from poorly passed-along narratives. If that's true, it would help to explain my obsession with seeing him honored and not forgotten; it would explain the tears I've shed for him. Maybe my tears are for a brother, a brother fallen stillborn from some common womb that I can't even name. Again, I don't know. My feelings, like so much in this brutal, beautiful, wounded world, are a mystery.

November 5th had been cold and cloudy, dreary in a Dickensian gray way. My visit with Price had been wrenching, sitting in the dirt at his grave, hot tears pouring from my eyes. I'd wept for him many times, but this was different; this was convulsive, consuming, complete. When I finally stood, I was drained.

I moved slowly back to where I'd parked among the huge gas tanks; from the beginning they'd born silent and stoic witness to my visits, my hopes and plans. I suddenly felt very alone in a way that I couldn't recall having felt before. As I turned the ignition, I remember hoping that Price was pleased.

And then the sun broke through the clouds for the first time in days, bathing the long lonely field in glorious autumn sunshine. The tiny graveyard with its grove of surrounding sentry trees lighted up in the distance like a beacon from forever ago.

I smiled weakly. There was one last matter.

James Foster is a friend of my daughter's, a former colleague in Purdue University's student affairs administration. She's referred to him as the kindest individual she's ever met, and her admiration for him is boundless. James is a black man in his sixties, now a fulltime pastor at his own little church in Lafayette. I met with him late in February of 2019; we discussed Price, what I'd learned about him, and my most recent realization.

"I'd like to have some kind of memorial service at the cemetery now that the stone's in place, and I think Price might like to see a familiar face," I stumbled, embarrassed. "Someone of color to speak the words. I think he'd like that."

James was reflective. For a moment I thought maybe I'd insulted him; I wondered if my thinking a black pastor would be a good idea was a kind of racist notion in itself, sort of like the serving staff I'd once seen in the great dining hall of the Grand Hotel on Mackinac Island: in an effort to preserve "historic authenticity," every individual was a person of color.

My concerns were groundless. "I think that would be entirely appropriate," James said softly. He was eager to perform the service. We talked more around the table there in his church, about how the service might look, and my motivations. We discussed the great rift between the races in our country and the need for dialogue and healing.

"It's not just having the conversation," he said. "We have to encourage the hope that needs to be in the room, the hope that things can actually change. We need to understand that *everybody* counts." He said he thought my efforts on behalf of Price and making them public were steps in the right direction. And not uncharacteristically I became tearful as I expressed my shame around my family's history of slavery and my own slow coming to awareness.

"I just had no idea how things have been for black folk," I said. "No idea at all."

James was quiet a moment.

"You know, I used to travel from Gary down to Bloomington from time to time." His voice took on the distant tone of someone recalling old memories. "My family warned me never to stop in Martinsville."

"Really?" I asked. "Martinsville?" I knew the little town south of Indianapolis. Nothing about it struck me as particularly remarkable; I'd passed through it any number of times commuting as a graduate student.

"Yeah," he answered wryly. "Bad things could happen to you in Martinsville."

All I could do was nod. I had no idea what that meant, no sense of the "bad things" that could happen to you in Martinsville. No idea, because I was white.*

As we parted that morning we hugged. We had the outline of a plan and agreed to select a spring date for

*Martinsville, it turns out, had a very robust Klan element in the early 20th century, even by Indiana standards.

the service. At our parting, he assured me that our working together had been "foreordained." I think I believed him.

Unknown to me, elsewhere, 2019 was being commemorated as the 400th anniversary of the beginning of slavery in the United States. In my part of the country, the morning of May 11 was gorgeous, cool and crisp with a brilliant sunlit sky adorned perfectly by wispy clouds. I stood with Peg, our children and daughter in-law, and some good friends in the little graveyard outside Acton, surrounding Price's headstone. James was there with his wife, as were reporters from the IndyStar, the local affiliate of USA Today.

A friend set the mood in his deep baritone, singing two acapella verses of *What a Friend We Have in Jesus*, the old hymn from the 1860's James had suggested. My son, standing near the graves of the men he'd been named for, read from the Book of Joshua; he'd chosen the King James version, the scriptures that Price and my ancestors would've known. My daughter recited Yehuda Halevi's poem, *'Tis a Fearful Thing*. And James delivered a beautiful eulogy.

He spoke of his gratitude at being asked to preside at the service, of Joshua's command to erect a stone monument that would serve as a perpetual reminder "to the people," of God's intentional creation of different races, of hope for our country. He spoke at length about Peggy's observation that "the beauty is in the fruit"- the fruit of God's loving care, compassion, the effort to stay connected, and most of all, the fruit of love. He expressed his hope that Price's stone would become a lasting testimony to the process of healing needed among the races in our society. And finally, with profound solace in his heart, he noted that while we may not know the details of Price's life, God most certainly did.

He ended with a blessing and our little group responded with a strong "amen." Price had now been laid to rest properly, memorialized and consecrated. As the group left the cemetery, I turned one final time to his headstone. "Price," I said, tears again in my eyes, "I love you."

One of the reporters asked if I ever pictured Price, if I ever imagined his appearance. I'd answered that while I often thought of him, I'd never been able to make out his face.

"Why do you think that is?" she asked. I had to admit I had no answer. I still don't. I think maybe that simply isn't the way my mind works: my reflections on the two century-old slave come to me in emotions and impressions, not visual images. But it pleases me to imagine that maybe someday it will be otherwise-

If I speak in the tongues of men or of angels, but do not have love, I am only a resounding gong or a clanging cymbal. If I have the gift of prophecy and can fathom all mysteries and all knowledge, and if I have a faith that can move mountains, but do not have love, I am nothing. If I give all I possess to the poor and give over my body to hardship that I may boast, but do not have love, I gain nothing.

Love is patient, love is kind. It does not envy, it does not boast, it is not proud. It does not dishonor others, it is not self-seeking, it is not easily angered, it keeps no record of wrongs. Love does not delight in evil but rejoices with the truth. It always protects, always trusts, always hopes, always perseveres.

Love never fails. But where there are prophecies, they will cease; where there are tongues, they will be stilled; where there is knowledge, it will pass away. For we know in part and we prophesy in part, but when completeness comes, what is in part disappears. For now we see only a reflection as in a mirror; then we shall see face to face. Now I know in part; then I shall know fully, even as I am fully known.

And so, there it is: someday, I hope, we shall see *face to face*.

Price and me.

Amen.

Appendix

Of Race Cars and Racists

I honestly didn't know my uncle well. My mother's only brother, he always loomed as a larger-than-life character for me. It seemed like my parents were always struggling financially, but my uncle lived in a sprawling many-roomed ranch house that boasted an enormous aquarium teeming with brilliantly-colored fish, a well-groomed garden walk with towering exotic plants and a bubbling coy pond, and an aircraft hangar in his back yard. The hangar was almost as large as the house, maybe larger, and from there he could taxi directly onto an airstrip and take off in his Bonanza six-seater, a plane he was fond of assuring us was the "Cadillac of private planes." Ironically, he always drove a Lincoln Continental, broad and imposing.

He was himself an imposing figure, tall and loud and ebullient. He loved to joke and tease, something, thanks to my extreme introversion, I usually found intimidating. Once, before Thanksgiving dinner, he delivered a prayer that must've lasted fifteen minutes, outlining the history of the holiday with names, dates, and locations. It was grand and ostentatious, like everything about him. My cousins (there were five) always had the newest and best toys. Visiting their house was an excursion to a noisy wonderland where there was too much of everything. My father always seemed dubious about the origin of my uncle's resources- after all, he was an automotive mechanics teacher in an inner-city public high school. But he always seemed to have the best of everything, and plenty of it. Dad gruffly theorized that my uncle was in debt up to his 6'4" eyeballs, but I have no idea.

My cousin once explained to me that his father had been sickly as a young man, and consequentially was unable to participate in sports. Instead, he reasoned, his dad got to tinkering with automobiles and found that he was good at it. My grandfather had been a pretty successful provider himself, operating a general store as a young man and then earning a degree in veterinary medicine, something that allowed him to work as a federal meat inspector during the Great Depression. He'd been able to keep his family quite comfortable when many others struggled to the point of desperation. His father's entrepreneurial spirit – and probably his money - allowed my uncle to open his own automotive repair shop and service station at a relatively early age. It was soon thriving and became a local hangout for the young men of the area. It was there that my uncle first learned of another group of young men racing automobiles in the Deep South.

It's the stuff of legend, the origins of stock car racing in that part of the country spanning the Carolinas to Georgia, but apparently it's mostly true. Moonshining had become a lucrative, if dangerous, profession during Prohibition and the Depression. An entire industry had developed souping up conventional passenger cars to deliver whiskey and outrun federal agents seeking to seize product and arrest purveyors.

It probably was inevitable in such a blood-churning industry that eventually the delivery guys would try to see whose car was fastest. Promoters soon realized money could be made in setting up racing spectaculars open to the public, but sometimes the very best drivers would be prohibited from entering due to liquor violations. The races proved to be extremely popular, but the crowds were often incensed that their favorite drivers weren't allowed to participate. Finally, one promoter from Florida decided to host races featuring the very guys who had been banned elsewhere. More than anyone else, "Big" Bill France, Sr., the eventual founder of NASCAR, can be credited with making modern stock car racing the entertainment behemoth it is.

No one in my family seems to know exactly how my uncle first learned of all these shenanigans, but he did, and in 1939 he towed his 1932 Ford roadster with its big powerful Mercury engine down through the Appalachian Mountains and along the Atlantic shoreline to Daytona Beach,

Folks had been racing next to the ocean at Daytona for some time; Bill France wasn't the first to do that. The beach itself almost insisted on it: at low tide it was uniquely broad and hard as concrete. Competitors had been pitting themselves against one another on the sand pretty much since the arrival of the automobile, and eventually drivers began swinging up onto the adjacent streets to form what amounted to a great circular road course. The first officially sponsored race was in 1936; in 1939 it was won by an unknown, an upstart from Indiana.

My uncle.

My uncle won the race at Daytona, and the impression he left on those southerners was permanent. He and Big Bill became lifelong friends, and when France opened the Daytona Beach International Speedway in 1958, a standing invitation remained open to my uncle and his family. My mother always seems somewhat enamored of Bill, Sr., and I have no idea at all if the feeling was reciprocated, but they remained in close contact until his death. She was deeply saddened at his passing.

You have every right to wonder at this point what this story, one of which I am rightfully proud, has to do with my present project. The answer is, frankly, mostly nothing, other than one sad adjunct to the whole affair.

I'd been aware for some time of my uncle's accomplishment and his relationship to the founder of NASCAR, and I also knew of a letter my uncle had received from France that testified to their nascent relationship. I'm not sure that my uncle ever returned to Daytona to race, but France had invited him to, which is what the letter's mostly about. I never saw it until a few years ago, when I came across it in my mother's possessions. It seems one of my uncle's sons, while managing a race track in Georgia, had given it to my mother. It's only a few lines long, and as I began to read it I felt a surge of pride...until I got to the end.

I want to be very clear about this: I *never* saw or heard anything in my uncle's behavior or conversation that indicated in any way that he was racist. He was the *recipient* of this letter, and I'm loathe to share it for fear of the likelihood that someone will implicate my uncle simply by reason of association. NASCAR, and motor racing in general, has often been accused of being racist, but I know nothing about that. All I know is what I read in France's missive to my uncle, and it too has become part of the permanent fabric of my family's history, for good or ill.

And so, I'll simply let the document speak for itself. Make of it what you will.

BILL FRANCE
AUTOMOTIVE SERVICE
AMOCO GAS & OILS

316 MAIN ST.   PHONE 9120

DAYTONA BEACH, FLA.

6/14/ 40

Dear Stew,

Just a line to say hello and send the entry blanks

See if some of the other fellows up there don't want to

come down and help you take home all the rest of the money.

Maybe you could find yourself

a good shop or gas station down south where a

nigger is a nigger and we make a living in our spare time.

So Long and let me hear from you

Bill

My grandmother's grandfather, Richard Alexander Stewart, was apparently made of grisly stuff. In a colorful short biography she wrote about him, my grandmother succinctly notes that he "drank vinegar in order to stay lean." Richard likely enjoyed the good things in life; his father owned a tavern and a large stable of racing horses. My grandmother describes their two-story brick home as spacious and filled with elegant furniture, including two large sideboards filled with bottles of fine wine.

Richard fell in love and eloped with the girl next door, Melinda, and they had nine children together. My grandmother recounts that one died at birth, one was killed in the Civil War, one died at two months of age, one died of measles as a young woman, and one died of pneumonia at sixteen. Only four of the nine survived their parents, and Melinda herself succumbed to tuberculosis, leaving Richard to remarry a woman named Elizabeth Riley, a cousin of the "Hoosier Poet," James Whitcomb Riley.

In her stories, my mother described the house Elizabeth maintained in grand detail. In addition to being roomy and opulent, it boasted a separate summer kitchen with an attic loft where chickens would occasionally roost and lay eggs. There was a brick two-room smoke house featuring an enormous black iron kettle. The images were so vivid to me I could smell the apples being squeezed through the cider press and the lard being rendered in the giant cauldron. Richard had been an avid horseman all his life, and apparently became a widely respected horse doctor of sorts, seeking out animals that had been poorly cared for and malnourished and nursing them back to health. In her writing, my grandmother talks of his feeding them "plenty of oats," and "when they became beautiful, he would sell them."

Richard Alexander Stewart with Richard Jr.

Horses were a vital element in the lives of these people and their neighbors; it's hard for us to imagine exactly how important they were to everyday survival. Horses provided personal transportation, movement of goods and supplies, and the power to pull the plows of agriculture. Horse thievery, because it was so lucrative and relatively easy, became epidemic, but it was regarded as a direct personal attack on the victims-catching and punishing the villains were seen as matters of self-defense. My mother took great pride in the fact that her great grandfather had been a duly deputized member of the "Hoosier Horse Thief Society," to use her words. In addition to tending to the medical needs of the local steeds, Richard had also been charged with seeking out the horse-snatching crooks and bringing them to justice.

But my mother abandoned her enthusiasm for her great grandfather's avocation after reading an article in our local newspaper about D. C. Stephenson, the notorious Grand Dragon of the Indiana branch of the Ku Klux Klan in the 1920's.

Stephenson, in his tenure as head of the Klan, became the most powerful man in Indiana, leading more than 200,000 Hoosiers and heading up Klan recruiting operations in other states. Every man who applied for membership paid a ten dollar fee, of which Stephenson took a cut. Originally from Texas, he'd made an unsuccessful run for Congress after moving to southern Indiana. But a mere three years later, he was commanding an "Invisible Empire" of thousands. He owned politicians, sheriffs, and businessmen; every third man in Indiana was a member of the Klan. He grew wealthy from graft, extortion, and in a brilliant move that prefigured modern merchandising, the sale of Klan garb and paraphernalia. He famously claimed to *be* "the law in Indiana."

And his law was enforced by none other than the Horse Thief Detective Association, his personal secret police.

To her great credit, my mother was nothing short of horrified when she learned about this from the newspaper article, which went on to detail Stephenson's eventual conviction on rape and murder charges. The Grand Dragon, while posing as a man of upstanding moral fiber and a strict Prohibitionist, had brutalized a young state worker after forcing alcohol on her, and his mistreatment eventually led to her death, a hellish, lingering process that stretched out over several days. Stephenson went to prison on a life sentence, but was paroled in the mid-1950's. His house in Irvington, only a few minutes' walk from where I currently write, remains a notorious monument to his power. It's said to be haunted.

The Horse Thief Detectives were nothing short of a terrorist group, intimidating (in the article's words) "Roman Catholics, Jews and Negroes." They stalked their victims, often beat them, and occasionally lynched them, but local law enforcement, sometimes Klansmen themselves, never seemed to notice. While my mother retained the article clipping in her archives, the subject of Richard Stewart's role as a Horse Thief Detective was instantly consigned to the great repository of things we never mentioned again.

I think, more than anything else, her reaction to the news speaks to the type of racism my mother harbored. Remember I mentioned that she wasn't a hateful, militant racist: my mother never would've endorsed anything so vile as lynching. Rather, she just truly believed that people of color were simple and silly and just not on a par with whites. They were *inferior*, but that didn't mean she wished to see them tortured and murdered. Her great-grandfather's association with the detectives shifted entirely from being a source of pride to one of shame.

But there's a wrinkle to this whole affair that I suspect exonerates my ancestor altogether. Mom not only kept the newspaper article, but she also kept Richard's original certification as a member of the group, the "Adams Horsethief Detective Association," Adams being the local jurisdiction in Decatur County that had issued the license. I can't make out the complete date, but it clearly says "1875," and, in those days – the days of Richard's membership – the group had no direct connection to the Klan at all, let alone to D.C. Stephenson, who wouldn't even be born for almost twenty years.

The detectives at that point in history were genuinely deputized constables authorized to apprehend horse thieves...vigilantes perhaps, but officially sanctioned ones. And just as the Klan of the 1920's had appropriated the titles and language of the Klan that had originated right after the Civil War, it had similarly appropriated the name of a once-legitimate arm of pioneer law enforcement, the Horsethief Detectives, to title its group of terrorist secret enforcers. My mother had innocently and erroneously conflated the two.

It only makes sense to me that Richard, with his abiding love of horses, should be inclined to try to root out the villains who stole them, and he would have been in a perfect position to make contact with anyone wishing to sell horses, purloined or otherwise. Many times the thieves would take their ill-gained goods out of state to make a sale; Richard would probably have known which horses were local and which were not. But there's absolutely no reason to think he might've been involved in anything harmful to blacks. At all. My mother's shame, in this case, was unfounded.

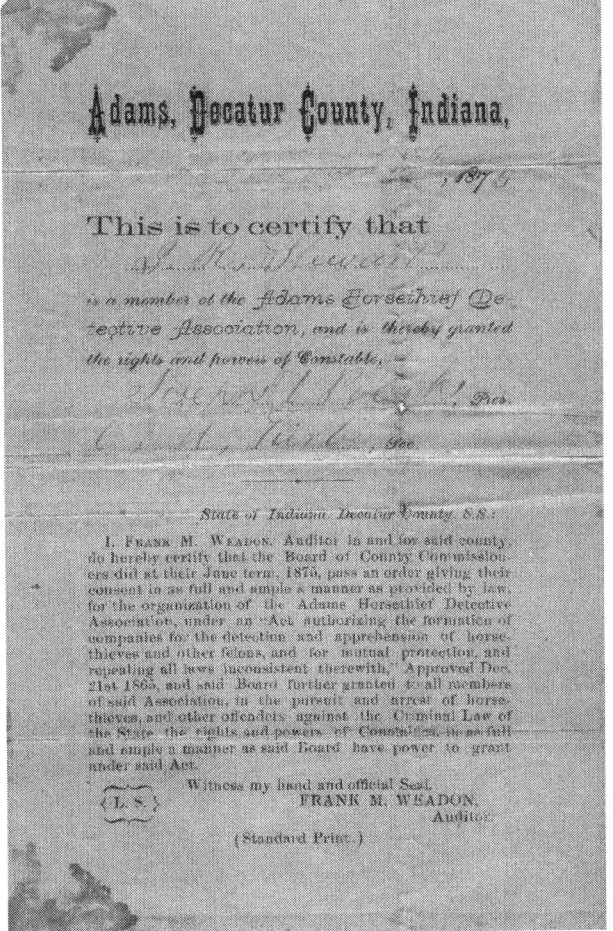

KNOLL FARM
Little Anti-Racist Library

**Please return or
exchange. Thanks!**

Made in the USA
Columbia, SC
22 July 2020